Praise for Deborah Heneghan and *Closer Than You Think*

"With a confident voice, a sense of humor, and wisdom borne of painful loss, author Deborah Heneghan speaks clearly of dealing with grief by trusting and learning how loved ones communicate and help us after they die. I couldn't turn the pages fast enough to read more miracle stories of how famous and not-famous people received endearing messages or how a deceased father pulled his famous son out of a burning car. Miracles happen, and we still grieve and feel pain for those we have loved and lost. Heneghan provides a voice of truth and inspiration to handle grief, accept life, and have faith in your continued connection and communication with a loved one. Her ten fundamentals are guidelines for healing yourself and helping others along the way. This is not another grief recovery book; this is a celebration of love and life in all realms, and I give it 10 stars!"

—Dr. Caron Goode, author of *Kids Who See Ghosts* and *Raising Intuitive Children*

"Fascinating new stories that show us life continues on the other side."

—Jacky Newcomb, *Sunday Times* of London, bestselling author of *An Angel Saved My Life*

"Once in a while a sleeper sneaks in—a book so unique it cannot be categorized. *Closer Than You Think* is just such a book. No, this is not the usual grief book on how to handle the death of a loved one. It is not even one of those stories about an individual on this side of the curtain channeling what a loved one says from 'the other side.' Such books have real value, but this one has more. Way more. Weaving all kinds of stories in and through her own, Deborah Heneghan covers every aspect of death and dying, life and living in a heart-filled, uplifting, and totally unique and wonderful way. What she has created is a caring and compassionate guidebook like nothing else I've ever read. She's done us a favor. She's opened up our hearts with this book . . . so we can see what's inside."

—**P. M. H. Atwater, LHD,** author of *The Big Book of Near-Death Experiences* and *Near-Death Experiences: The Rest of the Story*

"The perfect reminder that our loved ones on the other side are closer than we think. All you need to do is open your heart and mind to the signs and signals."

—**Jenniffer Weigel,** author of *I'm Spiritual, Dammit!* and *Stay Tuned*

Closer Than You Think

Closer Than You Think

The Easy Guide to Connecting
with Loved Ones on the Other Side

Deborah Heneghan
with Linda Sivertsen

Cover design: Nita Ybarra
Cover art: Chris Stein
Interior design: StanInfo

Hampton Roads Publishing Company, Inc.
Charlottesville, VA 22906
Distributed by Red Wheel/Weiser, LLC

ISBN: 978-1-57174-661-0

Printed in the United States of America

*In memory, celebration, and honor of my
beautiful sister, Kathleen Ann Wagner,
who inspired and guided the creation of this
book.*

November 8, 1969–February 21, 1987

Kathy, Honey, My Little Fuzz:

Even though you gave up your life when we were teenagers, you left behind countless blessings. Now it's my turn to give back to you. It's my honor—a true gift and blessing—to tell part of your (our) story, and to share with others how we've grown together and healed each other from one dimension to the next, despite our apparent distance.

I wouldn't be the person I am today—a fulfilled mother of two, a spiritual teacher, a successful businesswoman—if it weren't for you and our relationship since you journeyed back to heaven. I've never doubted that you left this physical plane to help those of us you love, from the other side. Your angelic imprint is everywhere and a constant in our lives. Thank you for caring for us so deeply and for being my inspiration, role model, guidance counselor, and my very best (Angel) friend.

I hope you enjoy this journey back in time for the purpose of helping others achieve what we have—a joyous two-way connection in which I continue your work here on earth (living for two, baby!), and you never cease guiding, entertaining, and blessing me beyond belief. You are my secret weapon, my staunchest ally, my heavenly eyes and ears. I'm extremely excited to share with readers all you've taught me so that they, too, can have what we have with their loved ones who have passed on.

I have experienced moments of intense pain as I've relived your passing for this book, but you've shown me over the years that it's all part of the canvas of a beautiful life. Death is, after all, a part of life for all of us. I've come to see that it's not some horrible end to be feared but a true beginning to be celebrated. Thank you for showing me how to celebrate life after life, to open my heart to love, and to profoundly understand the passing from this world to yours.

I love you so very much, my forever Angel sister. From my heart and soul to yours.

Now, let's go forth and spread a little of your stardust.

Love always,

GYB, Your Little Sis ☺

Contents

Introduction

Have you ever lost someone you love and wondered if she's trying to reach out, send you signs, or let you know she's okay? Have you hoped to establish a clearer connection with her? It can be remarkably easy when you know what to do. The payoff, as you'll see, is life changing.

I was fifteen when my seventeen-year-old sister died of Leukemia. A few weeks later, I woke up in the middle of the night in my pitch-black bedroom to a faint whisper summoning me . . .

"Deb, Deb, Deb."

I opened my eyes, and there she stood at my bedside. My eyes traced the outline of her body. Her thin frame was unmistakable.

It's Kathy! I thought. I had no doubt.

Trembling with excitement, I reached my hand out to try to touch her. As I leaned in toward her image, she vanished. In a panic, I jolted, fell back, and flew under my covers.

What did I just do? Did I scare her away? Is she okay? Is something wrong? Did she need something from me? Where did she go?

Seeing her, even for that moment, changed my life forever.

The next morning, confused but curious, I started talking to my sister about everything and anything. I continued this for days, and without realizing this was possible, the signs, messages, and answers to my thoughts and questions started flowing in.

When I needed confirmation of something, I'd flick on the radio and hear "Don't Stop Believin'"—her favorite song by Journey. I'd awaken in the middle of the night to see 3:10 on the alarm clock—her favorite number combination—with the big, bold, red digital numbers glowing brightly on the panel as if validating my question or concern. (I see this number all the time now—on license plates in front of me, on billboards or buildings on my way to work, or in glancing at my clock just when I need a sign. It's become our code and lets me know Kathy is watching over me.)

Little did I know at first, but we were establishing a method of communication between worlds. From time to time, I felt what I like to call an invisible hug wrap around me. My senses heightened, becoming more aware of these messages. Our conversations grew, and I talked with Kathy as if she were right beside me. I kept a log, a diary of sorts, of the most obvious angelic signs—something I'll teach you to do in Chapter 4 (I call it my Angel in a Pocket). Remarkably, Kathy and I built a trust between us, providing me with invaluable guidance and support as well as the confidence I needed to move forward. I like to think I also helped my sister fulfill unrealized dreams from her life. There was no question; this was a *new* relationship.

It's been over two decades, and Kathy's angelic imprint is still *everywhere* in my life, a constant. It's so obvious at times that it's downright comical. She's guided me into some of the best work and life situations I've ever experienced, *and* she's saved me from danger, once literally saving my life! Our relationship is a joyous two-way connection in which I continue her work here on earth, my own work expands, and she continues guiding and protecting me as my big sister. What started off as a bit of a lark—*living for two*—has morphed from the reaction of a heartbroken teenager to a lifelong practice. She never ceases guiding, entertaining, and blessing our family and me beyond belief. I never cease thinking of her and her dreams, and carrying her with me. Each of us healed through the other. I want that for you, too.

The powerful ways in which my sister helps me, comforts me, and communicates with me create a blueprint for you to follow. With this book, your relationship with your loved one can be one of the most fulfilling, protective, fun, natural, and beautiful things in your world—so much so that you'll believe, as I do now, that death is a beautiful part of life; a beginning, not an end. If that sounds too unbelievable from where you now stand,

I understand. Perhaps you're in a crisis of faith, as I once was. Losing someone near and dear to your heart challenges faith as nothing else can. I'm excited to share stories and techniques that have helped me and countless others restore and grow our faith, so much so that the first chapter is devoted to that subject. Also, at the end of each chapter, you'll find a core Fundamental to help you work through challenging situations and to keep you focused on your many blessings.

In case you're wondering, I assure you, I'm not one of those woo-woo types who sneezes rainbows and moonbeams. I do not have my head in the clouds. I'm a working mother with two young boys and stress like anyone else. I don't live in la-la land but rather in traditional Pennsylvania. I wear business suits, and I design software solutions for IBM. I teach tele-seminars and provide grief and life coaching to spread the profound healing I've received since my sister's death. I also enable people to find their way on their spiritual path through spiritual workshops and retreats and by sharing wisdom, experiences, and stories as an Internet radio host.

But for as much as I've found the blessings in my sister's death, I should also admit another truth: death sucks! Believe me, if I had my way and could reorganize the universe, I'd make sure no one would ever have to lose someone they love ever again!

The brutality of having to say goodbye to a person who gives your life meaning is unbearable. But because of how gut wrenching my sister's death was for me, because of how horrible and unfair it was for my parents and my other older sister, for my grandparents and Kathy's young friends—most of whom had never seen death—I *had* to find the silver lining. If not, I would have gone nuts, like my friend who used to wake up at night insanely trying to figure out ways to pull a Dr. Frankenstein and bring her father back from the dead. That's how crazy our minds get when we experience the inconceivable pain of loss. Even though I'm not a fan of the entire unfair system of death and grief, I've stopped trying to avoid and fight it. It's futile. After all, death has been around a lot longer than me, and it's not going away.

What might be comforting to you at this point is that no matter what kind of loss you're dealing with, whether it was an expected death from old age or disease, or a sudden, more dramatic death from an accident or worse, you'll receive tips and stories from people of all walks of life in a wide range of circumstances who have bridged the gap from here to there with heartwarming reports. No matter your situation, even if it's negative and you're dealing with unfinished business, anger, or a lack of strength, this book will help you regain hope. And although this may be hard to fathom, you'll also come to see that there are blessings and gifts that come with every one of your life experiences (even the dramatic and tragic ones). Finally, if you're already receiving signs and messages from your loved one and just want a few more fun ideas about how to deepen that connection, you've come to the right place. Love endures. And it's never too late.

I have the great blessing of helping countless people who have lost loved ones. It's something I've done informally since losing Kathy but now more formally as a grief and life coach. Whether I'm working one-on-one with clients, coaching a group in my spiritual workshops and retreats, or taking questions on my Internet radio show, I'm so grateful to be able to share what's worked for me while continuing to learn from the many others who have also turned their pain into peace.

What will you gain by reading this book? You'll acquire a sense of peace and validation that spiritual connections with the beyond occur each and every day, everywhere. You'll gain a newfound perspective on death and the grieving process. You'll begin to see and understand how to regain your faith, and interpret signs or messages that are coming in from people close to you who've passed on. Finally, you'll be inspired to dig deep, let go of painful blocks, and reignite your enthusiasm to live life on your terms, buoyed by heavenly support. And, even if you're not yet sure that connecting with loved ones on the other side is your kind of thing, this book will help you process your experiences and free up your energy for all of the good that's waiting to come to you and through you.

Closer Than You Think will touch and change your life if any of the following are true:

- You've thought about communicating, at some level, with a lost loved one.
- You've received signs, dreams, or other apparent messages, and have questions.
- You believe that death is tragic, unfair, or unacceptable.
- You're filled with anger toward God regarding your loss, and you want peace and healing.
- You're unsure about how to grieve or move beyond the grieving process.
- You've visited a third-party psychic in an attempt to find answers or healing regarding your loss.
- You ache to connect with your loved one without an intermediary.
- You want to celebrate your memories.
- You want to add more fun, gratitude, blessings, protection, and playfulness to your life.
- You want to move forward in your life while also keeping your connection with your loved one strong and everlasting.

I should say that this book is profoundly spiritual without being ideological. No matter what religion you practice (or don't), you will find much that speaks to you. If any part of the book feels a little *out there*, just take what feels right. You have my promise: if you keep an open heart and mind, you'll walk away with ideas you've never thought of, techniques that bring you peace (even excitement), and a renewed sense that everything happens for a reason and is part of a larger, benevolent plan. Then I know I've done my job. Scratch that. Then I know that Kathy and I have done our jobs, and that through her passing, the world is an even better place in which to live.

Yours,

Deborah (& Kathy)

⮜ 1 ⮞

Gotta Have Faith: Dumping Doubt Through Prayer

Faith. What does faith have to do with communicating with your loved ones on the other side? My experience is that no matter what religion you follow, practice, or don't, faith has *everything* to do with fostering a spiritual connection. There are countless things I could say on the topic of faith, but simply put—if you don't believe (have faith) that you can communicate with and receive signs from those on the other side, you won't. (Oh, they'll still send you messages. You'll just ignore them or attribute them to coincidence.) With faith, however, the possibilities are limitless. Your loved ones in spirit, no longer bound by the laws of earth, may just blow the doors off your limited thinking and your hardened heart.

But I get it. *Faith* can be a tricky word, and the act of being faithful, illusive. Let's break it down, shall we?

Faith. You hear it all the time, don't you? The word itself is bantered about like it should be the most natural thing in the world:

- Have faith.
- Keep the faith.
- *You've just got to have faith!*

But what if you don't have faith, or you've temporarily lost yours? What if you once felt faithful regularly, if not all the time, but after the loss of a loved one, you feel robbed of your faith? Faith is our natural state, but when we lose it with a loved one's death, we don't seem to be able get it back without going through the natural process of grieving (the topic of our next chapter). It's a must to work through whatever anger, depression, or pain has depleted your faith.

In this chapter, I share stories I've collected that are designed to inspire your faith, as well as a few considerations to think about anytime you're feeling low and need support.

First, I want you to know that faith waxes and wanes for most of us. Even Mother Teresa, through personal letters released upon her death, admitted being plagued by a crisis of faith throughout much of her life. When death touches you, as it did for Mother Teresa on a near-daily basis (as she administered to the sick and dying in Calcutta and some of the world's most impoverished locales for many years), it would be illogical to expect a person to have no doubts about the benevolence of the almighty.

I think we all ask ourselves questions after experiencing deep loss. Questions like: *Is there a God? Is God really a loving God? If so, why do bad things happen to good people?* And the big one: *If we're all going to die anyway, what's the point of life?*

I believe we're here to go through a variety of experiences (that *appear* both good and bad) to help us grow. If you're going through a crisis of spirit, my heart goes out to you. I understand what this kind of loss can do to your psyche and your view of life, God, and the Universe itself. Hang on. Things will shift. The feelings of hopelessness that often accompany grief do go away. My friend Linda used to describe the death of her mother as "the day the earth tilted on its axis," the day "nothing quite felt or looked the same way." While it took a year for Linda to feel the beauty of life again, no one could argue that her life wasn't forever altered. In her sadness, Linda never could have known that her mother was still with her and continued to enrich her life. She couldn't know that her belief in life would return. But thankfully, both proved to be true. As I believe they will for you.

My sister has been gone a long time now. I'm on the other side of grief, so you might think it's easy for me to be positive.

True. I have learned to look beyond her death as a sad, negative, and emotional situation and see it now as a blessing in disguise. But that takes time. And it's not always easy going. I do believe, however, that you will find gifts in death when you look deeply enough. It may take some digging, but gifts are there. Maybe it's as simple as recognizing your own dreams again, or listening to your heart. Remarkably, even after twenty-five years, I still discover new gifts from my sister's passing all the time.

Even when something doesn't immediately seem like a gift, my trust in life allows me to lift my head and stare down whatever has stepped into my path. What I've come to believe and experience over the years is that my higher power, God, never leaves my side. God guides me and loves me unconditionally, as He does each of us. Most importantly, God knows exactly what I need, when I need it, and how I need it. So, when a decision I made turns sour, or the outcome isn't remotely close to what I envisioned, or something happens out of the blue and the life of a loved one is taken, I believe that everyone involved is being led down a path for their highest purpose. It may take time to see how each experience actually helps me individually, but proof always seems to show up and put me back in my place; a good place—a place of 100 percent faith.

It's interesting to me that faith is universal. All cultures and religions throughout the world have a faith in God (or Gods), Spirit, or a higher power. All have a belief that the personality or the soul continues to have life after death. I like to think they're right. I cherish examples that remind me to dump my doubt and keep my faith. Like this one . . .

Synchronistic Street Fair

A dear friend of mine, Susan Kimutis—the author of *Receiving Birth*—and her husband, John, lost their nineteen-year-old son, Joe, to a tragic accident in March of 2011. As they were working through their grief, they began receiving signs of peace and comfort from Joe.

May the magic of the love that exists between worlds touch you through this story.

In Susan's own words:

One Saturday I was headed to my local health food store for a quick stop, but my plans changed when the main road was closed for a street fair. I weaved my way, blindly following the cars in front of me until I found myself again on familiar ground. I popped into the store, got what I needed, and was out. I had to park across the street in a funeral home parking lot because street parking was a premium, due to the street fair.

I called my friend Lisa and asked her if she was at the street fair and could she meet with me. She was not. I had no idea why I did that or why I stayed, since street fairs are not my thing. But I walked toward the center of town anyway, passing booths promoting the Rotary Club, the public library, and the funeral home, where I had just parked. I didn't stop. I was disinterested and soon decided to get back to my car and head home.

As I began walking back, however, I became slightly annoyed with myself because the new flip flops I was wearing were giving me a blister on the top of my foot. *What am I doing here? I don't even like Disney World; why am I at a street fair?* Those thoughts were hanging in a bubble over my head when I felt a tap on my shoulder.

I turned around to see a young girl, maybe nineteen, standing in front of me. She was holding a bright pink business card, which she quickly pushed into my hand. She had an accent and beautiful black hair. I was reminded of Joe when I saw her. "Would you like me to read your palm?" she asked. I hesitated, surprised. We discussed the cost and options, one palm or two. I decided on both palms.

The young girl grabbed my hands with purpose. She was pushing her thumbs deeply into my hands to better reveal every line. She began telling me a few facts about me. Yes, facts. Things about my life growing up. Then she did it.

"You have recently suffered a great tragedy," she said. "Someone very close to you has passed. Three of you have been affected greatly, but his passing has devastated many. Many, like a tribe of people. His life affected many." She used the word *tribe*, which I have heard *many* times describing the wonderful people who have circled my family since Joe's death.

"He is fine," she said. I realized in that moment that tears were running down my face, and I was not breathing. I took a deliberate, deep breath as she continued.

"Someone has been sad lately. He [Joe] knows this. He sees this man when he is sad. When the man is sad, he kisses the top of his head."

I started to get dizzy. The noise and commotion of the street fair was all around me. I was standing, growing roots in the center of the street, as this young girl continued to squeeze and look into my hands.

John had been having a difficult week. He was missing his beautiful boy. It was Father's Day. John was about eight inches taller than Joe. John was always kissing the top of Joe's head. I knew immediately what this meant.

Let me say that I, on occasion, dream about people who have passed. I am very open to everything she was saying to me. She could tell that I was open. She looked me in the eye and said, "You know this."

She then told me that he was watching very closely over someone who was younger than him but taller in this life. I knew of course, that was Sarah, his sister. She is 5'9". He was 5'7". He was fiercely protective of her.

"Please know he is fine. He is happy," the young girl said one last time.

We were done. I went through the motions of paying her. I continued crying as I walked back to my car.

When I got home, I gave John his Father's Day present from his son, who is fine, kissing the top of his head.

All is well.

Wow! Susan followed her inner guidance and found herself wandering through the fair, even though it wasn't something she typically fancied. The beauty of this story is that it's only one of many experiences that Susan, John, and other members of their tribe have been blessed with since Joe's passing.

They have faith. They are open. The grace of spiritual connections continues on and on for them, just as it does for Vicky in this next story.

Touched by Angel Clouds

My very good friend Vicky was in her thirties when she lost her mom to a sudden, unexpected heart attack. They were very close, and she was crushed to receive the call from her father late one night. Vicky hurried to the hospital, but she didn't make it in time. She tried moving forward from her loss by taking time away from her everyday life and booking a flight to vacation in Arizona with me.

We flew on separate planes, and during Vicky's four-hour flight, she sat in a window seat. A grandmother and the woman's four-year-old grandson sat next to her. The boy was outgoing and energetic—"as cute as a button," Vicky told me. He pointed out the window and, with such innocence, turned to Vicky saying, "There's an Angel out there. She's your mom. She wants you to know that everything is okay." Chills went up and down Vicky's spine. Tears poured from her eyes as she stared out the window, hoping to see this Angel, her mother. She saw nothing. The boy was surprised she and his own grandmother couldn't see what was right in front of them.

Although this child was only four years old, Vicky believed he was a wise soul. He did not give specific details about the Angel he saw, but he did say that she had a beautiful smile and was very happy." Vicky's heart exploded with love and appreciation. Since her mom had passed, Vicky always wondered if her mother was happy and at peace. At that moment, she knew. She cried and hugged the little boy as if he were her mom. The boy held her in his arms, comforting her, just as a mother would do. Vicky had faith the boy saw the truth, and she cherished knowing that her mother was happy and in a heavenly place.

Vicky, the grandmother, and the grandson spent the rest of the flight talking and getting to know each other. Once she arrived in Arizona, I picked her up at the airport and we headed straight to the hotel pool. It was a perfect, eighty-five-degree, sunny Arizona day. Vicky shared her story with me, and we laughed, cried, and reminisced. As we floated on rafts in the pool, gazing at the majestic mountains surrounding us, we couldn't believe our eyes. There, up in the crystal-clear, blue sky, were three perfect angel clouds, more intricate than any painting or drawing. One angel was playing a trumpet, another was simply flying through the air, and the last held a harmonica. We gasped, frozen in place, knowing exactly who those angels were—Vicky's mom, grandfather, and my sister.

We had never felt anything like this before. An indescribable calm, serene feeling came over us. More powerful than any connection we'd ever experienced.

Years later, Vicky still cherishes the bond she feels with her mom. "My mother has never left my side since. She has helped me through many challenges with her unconditional love and guidance whenever I need her."

I asked Vicky to share how she knows when her mother is nearby. "Oh, that's easy," she said. "I smell her favorite perfume when she's around, helping out." I thought about that, remembering a time another friend told me of smelling her grandfather's cigar in her apartment in college, the day she heard he had died, five hundred miles away. I hear that a lot from people—that they smell roses or perfume when a loved one passes or comes back from the other side with a visitation or a message.

"I also hear Mom's favorite songs when I need a hug," Vicky continued. "When I'm overwhelmed with feelings of sadness or anxiety, I will see her favorite movies on TV, even though they're oldies." Vicky knows it's more than the coincidences that make her certain her mother is sending her messages. "It's the feeling that comes over me when I smell, hear, or see these things. It's a peaceful, comforting feeling that washes over me, and it's very real."

It's the combination of signs and messages like these that continuously increases Vicky's faith, just as it does for me.

We all want to feel assurance from a departed loved one. We all want healing. People flock to dramatic signs that God or the Virgin Mary or Jesus or other saints could really exist in order to feel better about their place in this world. Thousands have reported seeing the Virgin Mary through apparitions in the sky, or they tell of seeing her statues weep, bleed, turn color, or move. Maybe you've heard of Lourdes, France, where five million pilgrims make the annual trek to visit the cave and drink the water where a peasant girl by the name of Bernadette Soubirous had eighteen Virgin Mary sightings in the late 1850s before she became a nun.

What I love about faith is that if you're open to believing, you can receive signs, or proof, that life continues after death *anywhere*, not just at a church or a sacred site far, far away. We are always getting messages from those who have passed on that they're here watching over us and loving us, even in the most unlikely places.

Restoring My Faith in Reality TV

I have a love-hate relationship with reality TV. I love getting caught up in these over-the-top shows, but I also think some of them go too far, disrespecting the participants and their audience. They can be incredibly shallow!

And yet, *The Bachelor* and *The Bachelorette* have been known to catch my interest—yeah, mine and about 15 million other Americans'! There was something very special and powerful about the last episode of *The Bachelorette* in the summer of 2010. Ali, the lucky lady doing the choosing, was standing at the altar in Tahiti, ready to proclaim her love for one of two men left standing. The man she did not pick, Chris (who had to pack his bags to go home with a broken heart), had previously shared his gut-wrenching story of quitting his job to help his father take care of his dying mother, a death that had only occurred within the last two years. Time and again, when Chris and Ali were together, he would speak of his mother and the wonderful relationship they had shared. He talked of the importance of family values and relationships.

During one episode, Chris mentioned that right before his mother passed away, she told him to look for her in rainbows—that she would come to him through them.

When Ali broke up with Chris, he was devastated. But there was a wonderful twist to the story. Not five minutes after Ali let him go, he stepped outside and what did he see? A huge, perfect rainbow! Chris was in awe, as was the audience, because it had not rained at all that day. All he could do was shake his head and look up to the sky toward his mother.

Ali had also seen the rainbow as she walked back to her hut. She, too, cried and smiled, completely astonished. She said she was so thankful that Chris's mom was there to help him through this trying time.

The best part for me was that the host of *The Bachelorette*, also named Chris (Harrison), talked about the phenomenon with the rainbow and how touching it was during the "After the Final Rose" show. He mentioned how everyone affiliated with the production of the show had acknowledged the rainbow and its connection with Chris and his mother, remarking at how amazing it all was.

I stood up and cheered. For a reality show.

Allow me to tell you why.

First, how many guys do you know who would feel comfortable spilling their guts about the death of a loved one during the first few dates with a woman? Second, how many guys even trust a woman enough to show deep emotions like this after dating a little while, let alone shortly after meeting her? I say not many.

Chris didn't hold back from sharing the story of his mother's passing, even though he was on *national* television and even though he knew he'd get very emotional. By exposing such a deep, emotional experience with Ali, I believe he energized his connection with his mother and opened himself up to receive a sign from her, even though he didn't realize a sign was coming.

The true miracle to me was the confirmation through media that life after death is real. The world has to change; something's gotta give! What better way to bring a little hope, faith, strength, and love to people than by touching hearts through a heavenly connection in front of millions of people?

Here's yet another example that touched the hearts of countless people around the world. This time I'll put a manly man spin on things.

Football Miracle

Maybe you remember when Packers quarterback Brett Favre's father died of a heart attack in December of 2003, just one day before a big Monday Night Football game against the Oakland Raiders. It was a big deal for sports fans.

Brett and his father were very well-known for their close father-son relationship. No one could believe Brett traveled to the game and suited up during such an emotional time. But what his fans watching him nationally and internationally *could* believe (and have talked about ever since) was how Favre passed for *four* touchdowns in the first half of the game, for a 41–7 victory over the Raiders. (Even hardcore Raiders fans gave Brett wild applause for his performance.) Favre's 73.3 percent completion rate for passing was the highest of his longtime career.

"I knew my dad would have wanted me to play," he said after the game. "I loved him so much, and he loved this game. It's meant a great deal to me and to my dad and my family. I didn't expect tonight's performance, but I know he was watching."

Those of us who saw Brett receive the award for the NFC Offensive Player of the Week before going to his father's funeral, and then go on to win an ESPY Award for that performance, had no doubt of his father's heavenly reach.

All I can say about these two widely publicized examples is *wow!* I thank God and the Angels for inspiring the world like this. It is time for all of us to realize just how powerful, beautiful, and easy it is to be inspired by and to connect and communicate with our loved ones on the other side. I can guarantee you that Chris found the strength he needed to mend his broken heart through his mother in spirit. I also believe Brett found the courage to face the world and play after his own heartbreak through his father in spirit.

When working with grief clients, I've found that it can help to use tricks, if you will, to kick-start a person's faith and hasten healing.

Here's a fun example—an exercise called **Automatic Dialoguing.** I'll introduce the idea with a little story written for this book by my friend and bestselling author Elizabeth Murray—an incredible painter, photographer, gardener, and writer from Carmel, California.

Elizabeth Writes to Gerald

In Elizabeth's own words:

On the fifth anniversary of the death of my beloved soul mate and husband, Gerald, I was in the Carmel Mission in candlelight listening to the sacred music of a choral group. I had brought Gerald here when he was quite ill and needed help walking. Leaning on the church pillar, not able to sit up straight, he said it was divine. Within weeks, his brain cancer doubled in size. Within a few months of outrageous suffering, he was transformed from a strong, vibrant, handsome, 6'4" man of great gentleness and intelligence to looking like a skeleton—tattooed from radiation treatments, starved from not being able to hold down food, his spark and vitality reduced to a shadow of my beloved groom. Only seven months after we were married, he was dead.

My grief was overwhelming, my questioning of every psychic, astrologer, and past-life reader enormous. I tried every which way to understand *why* he had died. We had met in college; he was my art teacher, and I was his favorite student. He was the first man to really *see* me and recognize me as an artist and encourage me. I fell in love with Gerald, but he was married and unavailable. We kept in touch, and twenty years later when his wife died of cancer, we were able to come together. Our love was fresh and deep and healing. It was new, yet contained lifetimes of familiarity and recognition. We believed we were soul mates who had found each other and had promised to be together. The depth of our love was palpable.

The pain of Gerald's illness was more than devastating. Yet there was always the hope that he would get better. God just wanted us to have a deeper faith. The garden we'd made for our wedding was to be a healing garden for others. We both had so much experience with death; we were going to help others through their healing journeys.

I've always felt like a healer—this time around, and I believe in many other lives. I long to be close to plants, to know the ways of nature, to bring comfort to others with rituals, teas, and cleansings. [Elizabeth is famous for helping to restore Monet's gardens at Giverny, and she has gone back every year for twenty-five years to photograph the gardens. She has sold over half a million books and calendars of this work.] I bring deep listening, loving acceptance, and compassion to my relationships. The love, beauty, prayer, and intention I showered on Gerald did not, however, mend his brain cancer. It raged on. I experienced a deep grief born of not only losing him and witnessing his suffering from the hands of the medical establishment, but of not being able to heal him myself. I know his journey was better for me being at his side, but this path was the hardest and required the most courage of any I have ever walked. His descent brought me to a crawl. Sometimes I curled up in wailing agony, as if scratching to break out of an eggshell that had me trapped in a cancer nightmare.

Five years after his death, I was beginning to heal and feel more "normal." I had finished my book *Cultivating Sacred Space* and was lecturing on love and loss. I had moved into my new house and had begun restoration work. On the anniversary of Gerald's death, two dear elders, Mr. and Mrs. Peck, were having a sleepover at my house for their sixtieth anniversary and had invited me to attend a concert at the Carmel Mission with them.

During the candlelight and sacred singing, I thought of Gerald and decided to see if I could communicate with him. I don't know why I thought of this, maybe because I love writing letters and had written many notes over the years. In my purse, there was a small piece of paper and a pen. I wrote some questions with my dominant right hand:

> *Dear Gerald, I love you. How are you? Do you have any guidance for me at this time?*

I answered with my nondominant left hand. This is what came through without any conscious thought:

Lizzie, I love you. I am so proud of you. You are doing so many wonderful things in your life. I want you to be happy. Thank you for all you did for me in my illness. I am sorry for the way the children treated you. I want you to love again. I will always love you, and we will meet again, but for now, be happy, believe in your wonderful self, and don't hold yourself back. I love your new house and all you are doing. Know you are always loved.

I allowed the pen to write without paying attention to how messy the words looked or what they said. I just kept writing until I was done. Then I would ask another question and get a few more lines.

The next morning at breakfast, I shared what I'd written with the Pecks, who had spent the night. They had no question that they, too, would be able to communicate after one of them had departed. They didn't think I was strange or weird, but felt happy for me that I had opened a direct way to communicate with my beloved Gerald.

A few days later, at home, I tried again. I sat in my rocking chair, looking out to the garden and some bamboo Gerald had given me, and wrote to him again.

Dearest Gerald, I feel so much better to be able to know you are all right; I wonder if you could give me some more insight and guidance as to what is the best path for me to take at this time in my life. . . .

Again sweet, loving, clear messages came through. Each time was like that. I didn't want to misuse this gift or bother Gerald—after all, he had died for a reason and might be busy. After some months, I began to ask my higher guides for guidance (Angels and people I loved who had passed on—my sister-in-law, friends, and more recently, my mother), and figured he could join them if and when he wanted. The answers were always loving and clear.

I don't know how this all works. All I know is that I am the scribe; I just write what I hear—kind of an intuitive message, word by word. I read it later and trust what I hear/sense and write that down, too. My writing is messy; I like unlined paper and a fast-flowing pen. I clarify my messy words or type my messages afterward.

Besides my friends the Pecks, I didn't tell anyone I was doing this for many years. Finally, I mentioned it to a dear artist friend who has traveled to the Amazon jungle with me twice and is quite spiritual and openhearted. I told her in almost whispered confidence—I was afraid of seeming too over the edge. Instead, Jody said that she, too, had done this type of writing before, having learned it from a PhD who has written books about dialoging with your nondominant hand. The idea is that by writing with your nondominant hand, you can more easily access your subconscious or your inner guides.

I am not sure who comes though for me, but I know for certain that it is a clear voice of wisdom, depth, and love. Specific information has always been clear and proved correct. I will even ask my guides what I should teach, what is the best topic for me to write about, or which workshop I should attend. I ask about decisions about my garden, or home or finances, as well as my love life and family matters.

———◆◆◆———

So go ahead—give it a try. The practice that has brought Elizabeth such comfort may provide you the answers you've been looking for. If nothing else, it gets you writing, which helps move the stale energy of grief. As you shift energy, you help open the doors to receiving answers and messages from your guides on the other side—and even your own inner wisdom. See what feels comfortable to you. No matter the method, I'm betting your faith will be refreshed from the responses you receive.

———◆◆◆———

One thing that always helps me feel more faithful is asking for help and receiving it. Here are a few stories that positively *filled* me with faith. (Plus, they're a good reminder to keep asking for help when you need it. I should note that it's also important to realize that you'll only receive guidance or answers when they don't interfere with life lessons you're here to learn on your own.)

Did Grandma Steal Those Signs?

Sandy, forty-two, was recently divorced and heartbroken about the thought of losing the home her daughters were born in. She didn't have enough money to stay put, however, and thus had no choice but to post for-sale signs in front of the house and throughout the surrounding neighborhood. Oddly, three different times, in three different locations, the signs were taken down—appearing to have been stolen. *Who would do that?* After months of painting, restoring hardwood floors, replacing hardware throughout the home, refinishing cabinets, combined with the ineffective string of back-to-back open houses (often without any signs), Sandy was at her wit's end.

Not one to often ask for help, Sandy broke down in bed one night and prayed to God and her grandmother for guidance. She prayed for support and the energy to get through this life-changing event for her girls. "Please just give me a sign that all is going to be okay!" Within moments, Sandy felt her hair being caressed. She couldn't believe the overwhelming calmness throughout her body. She could feel her grandmother right next to her, soothing her and providing comfort.

A few weeks later, as the saga of the sale continued on—and the signs continued to disappear—Sandy prayed and talked to her grandmother again. One day, out of the blue, a neighbor directed her to a financial analyst. Skeptical, Sandy placed a call, and to her surprise, a miracle occurred! The woman knew of a program Sandy had never heard of that allowed her and her daughters to stay in the house they'd always called home.

Was it Sandy's grandmother who had been taking down those signs, deterring buyers from seeing the house? Was it her grandmother who prompted her neighbor to provide the financial analyst's name? We may never know for sure, but there does appear to have been some type of loving, albeit mischievous and otherworldly, intervention going on.

I love this story. It has a happy ending, and it's a wonderful example of the power of asking for help. As we'll discuss in Chapter 5, if you don't ask, how do you expect to receive? Let go of any expectations of how your life should unfold. Being open to allowing *everything* to unfold in the manner it's supposed to means that you're truly letting go with 100 percent faith in the outcome. I've found over the years that holding on to a way in which something should or must play out is detrimental. Dissatisfaction will never bring you peace. And our way isn't always the best way, even though we think we know better.

Have faith that a power greater than you does indeed know what's best and in your highest interest. In order to arrive at those outcomes, you will be placed in different situations and experiences—some of them difficult—including losing loved ones. This helps you (and them) grow. Sandy eventually gave in to the possibility of staying put in her home, even though she was convinced she couldn't afford it. And although she was frustrated and disappointed during those many months, she followed the guidance that was provided and was pleasantly surprised in the end. In hindsight, she can see why it was so difficult to sell the house: because she wasn't meant to.

Letting go of expectations, being open to any or all possibilities, and having complete faith that everything will work out the way it's meant to will help you heal and move forward from any challenges you face. Sandy's grandmother didn't give the answers *to* Sandy; she merely provided the guidance to bring her to the best outcome for her and her daughters.

This type of support is life changing. I have faith our loved ones take great pleasure in intervening whenever they can. I speak from experience on this one.

Prayer Powered My Alarm

I have a house security system that alerts me when any door opens or closes throughout our home. With two little boys running around, this little precautionary step makes me feel more secure. The system is run by electricity, with a rechargeable battery backup. The battery itself only lasts several years, and it starts to beep loud warning sounds when it needs to be replaced.

The first time it alerted me, I had never needed to go to the main security box before and didn't know where it was. For days on end, I searched the garage and other areas of our home in an attempt to *stop* the dang beeping, which was periodic but always woke me up at night. No matter what, I could not find the main box. One night, the low-battery warning chime had been going off every ten minutes for over an hour already. I was exhausted.

I had had enough.

"*Please* recharge the battery long enough to last the rest of the night so that I can sleep," I said out loud to my sister and the Angels. "And *please* let me know where the darn security box is so I can get it fixed."

Immediately, and I mean at just that very moment, a thought popped into my head, telling me that the box was in the basement, by the hot water tank. There was a brief moment in which I wondered if it could *really* be by the hot water tank, but then I chuckled knowing that of course that was the location. Where else would a specific thought like that come from? Only from above.

Thankfully, the beeping had also stopped, so I lay back down and slept soundly for the rest of the night. Sure enough, when I woke up, I went right to the hot water tank, and there it was— the main box for our security system. What a blessing! This gave me even more assurance that our loved ones (and guides) are helpful even in situations that don't seem to affect our higher purpose. All we have to do is believe . . . *and ask!*

<hr />

Communicating with the other side is a joyous experience, which is why most of the stories in this book are light. But sometimes the tragedies we face in dealing with death seem too big to talk about, let alone overcome. And yet, people do it all the time. I've come to know several people, parents in particular, who lost children and yet still found the faith and courage to keep going (just as you read about

Susan at the beginning of this chapter). Because they were open, they were able to feel connected to their lost loved one in new ways.

Before ending this chapter, I want to offer you a more dramatic example that life goes on after death. It's a true tragedy turned sweet, and I hope it brings you more faith. Even though losing loved ones feels unbearable, it's actually those on the other side who can help you heal and find the comfort and strength to move forward.

Let's take a closer look at one such miracle—something that takes place all day, every day, worldwide, from big cities to small towns.

Tragedy Turned Sweet

Monique lost her daughter to a tragic car accident. Shortly afterward, her daughter came to her through subtle synchronicities, including many of the common signs we'll delve into later (through songs, animals, and dreams). Her daughter's essence also shined through during many uncanny comments and questions from her young grandchildren. From the combination of these happenings, Monique had profound feelings that her daughter was present.

Monique told me that she had been going through the normal, slow grieving and healing phases initially, but the moment she felt her daughter's presence close by, she said it was like an "instant healing," unlike anything she'd ever experienced.

Monique has a rare passion for life, and when we talk, I can feel the connection she has with her daughter radiate from her being. I'll never forget a few of the many words she shared with me, including:

"Losing my daughter, Nicoline, turned my world upside-down—initially it was awful. But I've come to learn that she isn't that far from me. She is as close as my next thought and always in my heart. Once I accepted that I couldn't bring her back, I realized just how close she is. In fact, this may sound crazy, but I'm so much closer to my daughter now than I ever was when she was here. Nicoline is a true inspiration to me, and her transition is a gift. My grief and sorrow started me on an inner spiritual journey. Without having experienced her transition, I might not have looked beyond my physical shell to what's really inside of me—love for myself and for all. And because of this, I'm now pursuing what makes me the happiest in life. I have my daughter to thank for giving me the strength to do something I've wanted to do for a very long time, but never had the courage to do.

Monique is not the first person who has told me of feeling a stronger connection with a loved one now that they're on the other side. And she's not the first to tell me that she's gained a newfound sense of her own power through knowing how well she's loved and protected.

———◆———

Before ending this chapter with a few key reminders, I'd like to say that over the years, after looking back and evaluating the challenges in my life and how I've overcome them (as well as providing help and guidance to my clients with their situations), I've identified core themes that I call **Fundamentals.** These Fundamentals are helpful reminders when working through any challenging situation. You'll see a specific Fundamental at the close of each chapter—one that corresponds with the topic discussed. Use them to help you move toward a more spiritually fulfilling, connected life.

The First Fundamental: Faith

One of my favorite **Fundamentals** is **Faith.** Here are a few things to remember about this powerful act.

Tips and Considerations for Keeping the Faith

- Faith is within you, always. Look deep inside (or all around you), and you'll see and feel it when you're ready to accept its healing embrace.
- Seek to understand what's causing your lack of faith. Have you fully grieved the loss of your loved one, or have you shut

down your feelings? As you'll see in the next chapter, when you release your emotions, you shift your energy from dark to light.

- Have faith that although you may be living with great pain—and can't in your wildest dreams imagine how this could be good for you—trust that one day you'll understand and clearly see exactly why things have happened the way they have.
- Keep your chin up! It took me some time to build up the foundation of faith I now depend upon. My faith grew and deepened because I looked back and recognized the blessings in my pain. I attribute my deep faith to the beautiful connection I have with my sister. Who might you communicate with to help restore your faith?
- Finally, have faith that every experience in your life is a necessary stepping-stone for all the good that's ahead of you now.

Good Grief: Let 'er Rip; It's Better Out than In

Losing someone near and dear to your heart is one of the most difficult experiences you will ever endure. There is no definitive way to get through it. Everyone grieves in her own time, at her own pace.

In this chapter we're going to take an in-depth look at grieving—what it is; how (and why) to go for it to get it out of you; how long it lasts, and how long is too long before you might expect to feel happy again. Even though there is no right or wrong way in which to grieve, it is very important *to* grieve. Only then can you turn your pain into peace—my main goal in writing this book—and experience your life to the fullest.

If I've done my job, the stories shared in this chapter will give you a new perspective on death and grieving, and a sense of calm and comfort that will make all the difference in your time of loss.

It's Harder for Those Left Behind

In 1988 actress Jane Seymour had a near-death experience—a by-product of taking bronchitis medication. She left her body and floated to the ceiling, looking down and watching as a team of doctors raced furiously to save her life.

"I did not want to go," she told Linda Sivertsen for *Balance* magazine. "When I found myself literally out of my body, I

thought, 'No, I have children; I have things I want to do. . . .'
I was thinking about my children and about wanting to give
back. When I did come back into my body, I was so grateful to be
alive that I began giving an inordinate amount of time to charity
work, which I still do."

When asked if she was able to transfer the calm she
experienced on the other side to her everyday life, she
replied: "Oh yes! Now that I know what death feels like, I
know that it hurts more for the people who are left behind
than it does for the person who is dying. I know the body isn't
who I am; what I am exists outside of it. So, I not only take
good care of my body, by eating healthfully, exercising and
getting plenty of sleep, but . . . I go with the flow. I know that
even if something looks like a struggle, which it often does,
everything will work out."

I tell you this story not to try to prove life after death or
reincarnation or anything else. I repeat Jane's account because it
echoes those of countless others throughout the world who speak
of their near-death experiences as being anything *but* scary. Over
and over, when people wake up (otherwise known as coming
back into their body), they report that instead of the terrifying,
painful, or tragic event we imagine, the actual moment of leaving one's physical form is filled with immense love, light, peace,
beauty, and comfort. (As many as half of recorded near-death
experiences, according to certain studies, reveal that deceased
relatives were present to greet them and even hold them back
from going too far away from their bodies when their excitement
took over.) The overall positive nature of these reports may not
make you miss your loved ones any less, but if you're having
trouble letting go because you saw them suffer and worry they
may not indeed be in a better place, it might help you to think
that the only true suffering surrounding death appears to happen
down here on earth.

I, like so many of the bereaved, suffered unnecessarily when
my sister died, worried sick that she might still be in pain somewhere. But over time, with an open heart and mind, I started
to give myself permission to grieve and therefore to trust. As
I experienced the magic of Kathy's presence and witnessed

similar miraculous happenings in the lives of people around me, I became all that much more convinced in the power of spiritual connections.

Grief Hurts

I should say, too, that not everyone experiences grief after the loss of a loved one. And that's okay. There's nothing wrong with you if you don't end up falling to the floor in a puddle of tears at the news of your Aunt Gertrude's death. We all have differing beliefs and emotional ways of processing what surfaces. What brings one person to her knees may barely affect another.

Sometimes, too, death brings relief, even joy to those left behind. If, for example, your loved one has suffered through a long illness, has been given time to process her life and death, has said her goodbyes, and is emotionally ready to go, her passing—while still sad—may leave you with a feeling of thanksgiving. She's no longer in pain, and life can start getting back to a new normal for everyone involved. Certainly when an older person who has lived a good life dies peacefully in her sleep, there can be a sense of right timing and good fortune for family members who might feel grateful their loved one will never endure the hardships that so often accompany old age and death.

But for many of us dealing with the loss of a loved one, the experience leaves scars. Even though the focus of this book is on the many blessings surrounding death, including those from seemingly tragic circumstances, that doesn't mean death doesn't suck! Losing someone you love is never easy and shouldn't be dismissed as anything other than what it is—a *very big* deal! In order to get through it, you have to *grieve* through it—even if your loss was years ago. Grief, like an onion, has multiple layers.

Rather than pretend that my sister's death didn't happen, or sleepwalk through my grief, I ultimately looked death square in the face and confronted my anger, fear, and loss. Only when I felt, processed, and fully let go of the mix of my emotions did I transition from pain to peace. I don't want to make it sound like a piece of cake, because it was far from it. My point is, if you don't allow yourself to *feel* your emotions from your loss, you'll keep yourself from moving forward in a healthy manner; or worse yet, you'll get stuck in a rut of grief.

You may still have zero or very little faith in a higher power. After all, why would a loving God take your beloved from you? Why does life—your life—have to be so tragic? Hopefully Chapter 1 helped provide you with a bit of comfort. Maybe your anger is already subsiding and that grudge you've got against God is starting—even ever so slightly—to make way for the restoration of your faith. I hope so!

For now, it's important to realize that however you've been responding to grief is normal. Depression, sadness, loneliness, withdrawal—you name it—someone is experiencing it right now right along with you. In my sister Cindy's case, as you'll read about in this next story, it's not uncommon for people to simply continue on as if nothing ever happened. But that doesn't mean that their insides aren't tearing them apart and that the negative effects of burying their emotions aren't bubbling up in how they live.

The Chip on Cindy's Shoulder

Cindy was tough as nails on the outside. She believed that, as the eldest in our family, she had to be strong. Over the years after Kathy's death, Cindy experienced a lot of turmoil. She often argued with people. She created drama in her life with such regularity that it looked, to me, as if she was trying to stay busy and dance around the real issue—her pain. There was no getting through to her. She wasn't open to therapy, spirituality, or anything that required her to let her defenses down.

I used to see Cindy watching me out of the corner of her eye when I'd talk to others about my two-way connection with our deceased sister. If she ever wanted to try to establish contact herself, she sure never showed it. Cindy wasn't one to ask for help, not for anything.

Cindy was relieved to see Kathy no longer suffering, but she was very angry that Kathy had been robbed of a full life. We were both furious at the Catholic high school Cindy and Kathy attended because they weren't supportive of Kathy during her battle with leukemia and didn't help our parents by supplying a tutor when Kathy was bedridden. Cindy couldn't reconcile in her mind how an institution that's supposed to support its followers in need offered far less than the free public school we ended up transferring Kathy to instead.

Because she never processed her anger, Cindy shelved it and ignored her rage and fear, living as if she hadn't indeed experienced the biggest trauma of her young life. A few years later, the two of us got together to create photo albums and videos for our parents' sixtieth anniversary, and Cindy broke down for a millisecond and cried. Then I watched as she turned off the valve to her feelings and said, "Okay. All done now! I have to be strong!"

As Cindy continued to live a chaotic life, she simultaneously watched me experience daily miracles and talk with our friends about the angelic blessings I was experiencing. Little by little, she started to open up. I think she saw that I was happier and more positive than she, and she wanted that. I talked with her about accepting our sister's death and went so far as to suggest she talk to Kathy to see if doing so would help her break through some of her blocks.

Cindy started praying to Kathy and God, asking for help. At first, she felt as if she had to move mountains. But as she slowly began to grieve and let out her angst, Cindy felt more supported and more comfortable expressing herself. She saw and felt real results. Today, five years later (and twenty-five years after our sister passed), she prays all the time and reaches out to our sister like it's nothing. "Life is just better this way," she says.

Maybe you've experienced a similar situation, in which life feels a bit more difficult, negative, or harsh, and you wonder if it's in part because of your defensiveness or aggressiveness. Perhaps you feel like every time you resist something—maybe the situation or your feelings about it—the negativity only continues to persist.

Typically, when clients of mine are experiencing these dark energies, we find that they've been burying their emotions. Emotions need an outlet. Otherwise they'll eventually burst, like a balloon does when given too much air. When Cindy began releasing her pent up energy and emotions by chipping away at the mountain of her defenses and asking for help, her life changed.

Kathy Comes to Cindy!

It wasn't until Cindy had become a believer that Kathy appeared to her. One night, not long ago, Cindy found herself overwhelmed with the dating scene after a divorce. She was lonely, afraid, and questioning her decisions. She couldn't sleep and got up to go to the bathroom, catching a quick glimpse in the mirror. There was a girl that looked just like our sister—with a slim build and short hair, just like she'd had following her chemotherapy.

"I felt an immediate sense of peace and calmness," Cindy said. "I couldn't believe she came to me!" Cindy crawled back into bed and felt so relaxed, as if she were being rocked to sleep. A few days later at bedtime, Cindy took out her contacts, as usual, and went to sleep. She's blind as a bat, but she woke up at 11:11 (a spiritual number in numerology) and could see the clock as though she had perfect vision. She took notice of this because the numbers "jumped out" at her. She went back to sleep and woke up a second time to numbers that again leaped out at her—3:10 (remember, Kathy's number). When she fell back to sleep, she had a glorious dream of our sister visiting. In it, Cindy was lying on a couch on her left side, and Kathy came to her and lay down next to her, cheek to cheek. Cindy felt immediately protected and loved. "It felt like she was saying, 'Don't worry, you're protected no matter what decisions you make.'" Cindy woke up feeling peaceful and wonderful.

Wouldn't you know it? Cindy now sees signs all over the place—numbers, birthday greetings, song titles speaking to her, birds delivering signs (something we'll talk about in Chapter 6), and so on. She's elated by the connection she's formed with Kathy and the world of beauty their union has opened up for her. Her joy reverberates through our whole family—literally healing stress we all carried as a result of her unhappiness. My sister went from Ms. Hard Ass to Miss Open Heart, regularly showing her emotions and being a comfort to be around. It's the most amazing transformation I have ever been blessed to see.

This experience showed me that we really are all on our own timeline. There is no right or wrong way to grieve, no perfect or imperfect time in which to get it done. But if you'd like to shortcut your process and add light, ease, and joy to your life, maybe learn from my sister's experience and don't wait twenty-plus years before doing your grief work. Cindy had struggled to build a life on top of years of unexpressed pain. That's no easy task. We all talk about how much easier we think her life would have been had she been open to receiving help many years earlier, possibly even as a teenager, as I did.

So, Let Me Ask You . . .

Are you currently grieving? If you're not so sure, read through the list below and see if you're experiencing any of these feelings in connection with the death of a loved one. If so, I've got news for you, this just means you're human and hurting. In other words, welcome to Griefsville, my friend.

Intense sorrow	Despondency
Heartache	Misery
Anguish	Hopelessness
Profound Pain	Despair
Angst	Dejection
Misery	Depression
Overwhelming Unhappiness	Discouragement
Woe	Melancholy
Deep Sadness	Suffering
Distress	Torment

Okay, so you're in it. Now what? This is your lucky day because I've got a few ideas. ☺ First and foremost, I'm going to ask you to do something that might be very uncomfortable: go for it and really purge your pain. Get it up and out. Give up the "ugly cry," as Oprah says. That might mean screaming into a pillow or crying in your car. It might mean writing that person a long goodbye letter or an apology one instead. It might mean booking a therapist appointment and baring your soul to a trained grief counselor. But whatever you do, play full out. Let 'er rip, potato chip.

If you're asking why—as in, what good could possibly come from allowing yourself to relive such agonizing pain?—I say this . . . it's only going to get worse. What doesn't come out now doesn't go away. Emotional pain gets stored in our bodies, hearts, and minds. And over time, that muck and mire can cause you more heartache, even illness.

The Yoda of Grief

The best information I've ever heard on the topic of grieving and what happens when we don't do it comes from a retired cop turned public speaker and therapist for police officers, Bobby Smith, PhD. Bobby knows more about grief than perhaps anyone, having learned about it intimately, far sooner than one should have to. As a toddler, Bobby watched his mother suffer a horrible illness that eventually took her life on his tenth birthday. As a Louisiana state trooper—a job he adored for eleven years—he was shot in the face and blinded in both eyes by a drugged-out, wannabe cop killer at a highway checkpoint. In the hospital, blinded for life and overwhelmed with depression, he learned that his wife was having an affair and had taken most of his belongings. Later, while living alone and forced into early retirement (which, by the way, didn't cover all of his bills, forcing him to move), Bobby learned that his only child at the time, his beautiful teenage daughter, had been killed in a car accident. I could go on from there, but it's not my intention to cause you stress. It's interesting to note, however, that as easy as it is to get into victim mode and feel sorry for yourself, when you think you've got it bad, someone else always has it worse.

I'm about to share Bobby's philosophy on getting over loss with you because of how well it works. The proof, as they say, is in the pudding. Bobby laughs more than anyone you'll ever meet—the kind of contagious laughter that comes from deep down in his core. He met and married a beautiful woman, and they have a very successful life despite the hardships he's endured. As the most popular law-enforcement speaker in the world, his stories move countless people every year. Bobby takes a room filled with hundreds of big, strong police officers and, in the span of ninety minutes, has them bawling like babies and then gut laughing, often with happy tears rolling down their faces. The experience is not to be missed.

One of the things that resonate with cops is the idea that they don't actually have to be superhuman. In fact, it's not possible. Think about the job of a cop. They're supposed to protect and serve (thereby staying *strong*) while witnessing, sometimes on a daily basis, the worst things imaginable—child abuse, suicides, homicides, drug addiction, animal cruelty, fatal car accidents involving babies and children, and so on. The onslaught can and very often does wreak havoc on their emotions and relationships. Bobby teaches that unless officers who are holding all that stress cry and experience their pain, and have an outlet, such as exercise or talking with others, their emotions are held hostage, locked up inside. Over time, that stress compounds and creates all sorts of inappropriate and misplaced rage, addiction, illness, and self-sabotage. That's why Bobby says the divorce rates for cops are off the charts, as are the rates for addiction, domestic violence, and suicide.

You Cannot Heal until You Feel

"Feelings are like taxes," says Bobby. "You either deal with them regularly or pay dearly down the line, with interest!" He remembers an old Fram oil filter commercial, in which a mechanic stands in front of a smoking automobile with an orange oil filter in his hands. He's trying to convince a customer to spend a little money now to put in a new oil filter instead of spending a lot of money later when the engine starts smoking. The mechanic says something like, "You have a choice. You can pay me $2.50 now (pointing to the filter), or you can pay me $2,500 later (pointing to the burning engine)."

I love that story and wholeheartedly agree.

I don't know where we got so off track as a society when it comes to expressing our emotions. In the book *Crying: The Natural and Cultural History of Tears*, by Tom Lutz, the author writes that it was common for both men and women to cry openly prior to the Industrial Revolution. (That makes sense, doesn't it—that we all had to toughen up to handle the hours of working like dogs all day long in factories, miles away from our families. I admit I don't cry much at the office either.) Lutz writes, "Heroic epics from Greek times through the Middle Ages are soggy with weeping of all sorts." He says that when Roland, the most famous warrior of medieval France died, twenty thousand knights supposedly wept so profusely they fainted and fell from their horses.

Bobby Smith loves a good cry, as do I, and believes it acts like good medicine. In his bestselling book, *The Will to Survive: A Mental and Emotional Guide for Law Enforcement Professionals and the People Who Love Them*, he tells a story about sitting in a hotel room preparing for an eight thirty a.m. lecture. Having turned on the TV to occupy his mind before going to speak, he realized he'd turned to a show he'd seen many times prior to his shooting—a show about family, character, integrity, and the importance of loyalty. It was *Little House on the Prairie*. You might remember Michael Landon's character, Charles Ingalls, or Pa, the lovable husband and father, but you may not remember his sidekick, Mr. Edwards. Mr. Edwards was a rough mountain man—loud, obnoxious, and Charles's best friend. The dialogue between the two characters caught Bobby's attention as he walked back and forth getting dressed, and he sat down on the edge of the bed. He listened intently as Laura Ingalls talked lovingly with Mr. Edwards about why he had just called off his engagement with a woman many years his junior, with whom he was very much in love. Their conversation went something like this:

"Mr. Edwards, why have you called off your engagement when you love her so much and she is so much in love with you?" Laura asked.

"Well, I'm just an old man, and it's not fair to her because she's so young and beautiful. I'll probably be dead before she even reaches the prime of her life, so it just wouldn't be fair to her."

"Mr. Edwards, are you sad?"

"Yes, I'm very sad," he said.

"Do you want to cry?" she asked.

"No. I don't want to cry," he said. "I want to laugh. But I know before I can ever laugh again, I must first learn to cry."

"I rose to my feet," Bobby writes, "pointing at the TV with my right hand, damn near spilling my coffee. 'Mr. Edwards,' I shouted, 'that's what I've been trying to tell them for ten years! That's what I'm about to lecture on to a room full of police officers! That's what I'm *always* trying to say!'"

Somewhere on some studio lot decades ago, a writer knew the perfect thing for Mr. Edwards to tell Laura, showing Bobby that the writer understood a thing or two about dealing with loss.

"You cannot heal until you feel," says Bobby now. "No one can."

I couldn't have said it better. I suggest writing Bobby's quote on a Post-it note and sticking it on your mirror, putting it in your wallet, or making it the screen shot on your iPhone. If you place it somewhere handy, you'll have a visual reminder of the power of letting out your emotions—one of the key ingredients to a healthy life.

Looking in the Rearview Mirror

Before you can deal with your present, you have to deal with your past. Bobby and I believe you cannot heal from the losses you've experienced until you feel the pain and sadness connected to *each* and *every* event. We're not just talking about the death of a parent, sibling, or spouse here. We're also talking about the death of your first dog, moving away from your best friend, the divorce of your parents, the flood that ravaged through your town, your high school heartbreak, and the death of a grandparent.

Acceptance is the key that makes it all possible. Delving into your emotions may mean that you become angry with yourself or the people you love. But time does heal the deepest of wounds. When you're willing to face your grief, when you're willing to accept what is, in time, your anger will turn to understanding and forgiveness. You don't have to like your losses (Bobby will never like the fact that he's blind, that his mother died on his birthday, or that his daughter passed away before reaching adulthood), but the path to healing is through acceptance—a learned skill that comes only from doing. The more you courageously face your losses and *accept* what is, the more you will heal and the happier you will be.

Grieving Doesn't Have an End Date

I would *love* to tell you that there's a designated starting point and a clearly marked end date to kick this grief business in the you know what. When that date would arrive, you'd be all done—never again to shed even a tear. Lord, how I wish! No more anguish. No more crying. No more depression.

That's just not realistic. Most things heal with time; other things will never totally disappear—the emotional strain of a disability, for instance, or the death of a beloved. While time heals most of our wounds, some scars remain. In Bobby's case, he's learned to live without sight, but every time he goes outside and feels the warm sun on his face, he's reminded that he hasn't seen anything but darkness in decades. He's reminded of his limitations and has yet another opportunity to learn to live with his loss. But he takes that opportunity every time, because he feels and processes each emotion as it surfaces.

What to Do if You're Still Hanging On

It's common, from time to time, even after you've done your grief work, to want to go backward toward what's familiar and pull the blanket of grief back over your head. For some reason, especially when we're particularly tired or stressed, we desperately want to stay connected to those we love. We miss them and therefore want to hold on. We ache for just one more moment in their presence, and we slip into woulda-coulda-shoulda thoughts of how things should have gone differently. Or sometimes we feel guilty for being happy.

Denial and anger are natural bedfellows. As much as you may want to grieve, doing so is often initially painful, thus understandably avoided. Many seek help and guidance from psychics, mediums, priests, or other third parties to provide them with at least one more chance to talk with their loved one to get answers about what happened, why, or what's next.

I would have gone to a thousand psychics if I'd thought it would have brought Kathy back or helped me talk with her. But I stumbled upon the possibility of doing it on my own when I started talking with her directly. Sure it felt odd, forging a relationship with a person no longer here in the physical form. But talking with Kathy made me feel good. Twenty-five years ago, I would never have dreamed I'd recommend such craziness, but I liked how relieved I felt after getting things off my chest. I became accustomed to how peaceful I felt every time Kathy seemed to send me a sign.

Now, after countless instances of proof that Kathy continues to exist happily somewhere else and yet still delights in making my life on earth not only safer and more abundant, but also funnier and more exciting, I would say that, along with the birth of my children, my sister's passing is the most glorious gift I've ever received. I no longer see her early death as tragic. I no longer feel anger or grief about how she was taken so young. Instead, I see her death as a powerful part of our life path this time around, something that has empowered me, heightened my intuition, and expanded my vision of what I'm capable of and what it means to be alive.

The Gifts that Keep on Giving

The death of a loved one can be an invaluable wake-up call that helps those left behind get on a better path. Sometimes our loss—as hard as it is—affects us and inspires us to do something we'd never do otherwise. I've been blessed to know wonderful people who have faced unthinkable pain. Two in particular lost their children to tragic accidents. But it was because of their loss that they changed careers. It was because of their loss that they became more spiritual. It was because of their loss that they became more loving and compassionate. It was because of their loss that they were able to start enterprises, teach others, write books, and counsel parents going through similar pain. It was through their loss that they touched the hearts of many others and changed lives for the better, forever. These are a few of the gifts available to us all the time.

If you're having a hard time seeing the gifts in your loss, be patient with yourself. When you can, take a moment to look beyond just you. Is it possible that the death of your beloved has brought an extended family member or members back into the fold? Is it possible that their death has erased old hurts or grudges within the family that had been infecting the love for years? Is it possible that this death has given someone close to you a nudge to do what they've always dreamed of doing but were too fearful to try? Is it possible . . . be open to the gifts and blessings from your loss.

The Second and Third Fundamentals: Surrender and Release

The key **Fundamentals** for this chapter are **Surrender and Release**. Grieving is the most important step to freeing yourself from the pain of loss. As you feel your feelings—whatever they are—and give them room to breathe, you're able to surrender your fear and release their toxic grip. It's like shining a light in a dark room to reveal the beauty that has always been there, only hidden from view. Be patient with yourself and know that you deserve help whenever you need it. You deserve to feel free and happy. Your loved ones want the world for you. Show them that you're ready to surrender and release your pain to receive all the good they have coming your way.

So how do you begin to work through your deep emotions and heal? Here's a brief list of what I do. See if any of these help you.

1. **Stop and feel your emotions every day** so that you're free to move forward. (Burying them with TV, food, anger, sleep, or some other addiction will only ensure that they come back stronger.) If you have a difficult time processing emotions through speech, try writing. Grab your journal and write your heart out about your frustrations, your anger,

your guilt—whatever! You'll find as you write, words spill onto the page. When you're done, rip the paper to shreds (or safely burn it) with the intention to move forward with ease. By feeling your emotions and getting them up and out of you, you naturally shift the energy without having to intellectually figure out how to heal. It's a natural process of letting go.

2. **Go for a drive and scream** at the top of your lungs about how unfair life is. No one's around to hear you, so this is your chance to be loud and to air your grievances. Don't worry. You'll get back to being positive later. (Be mindful of the road, however. I usually park before I get too emotional.)

3. **Watch a favorite movie** (or your loved one's favorite), or even a tearjerker to help unfreeze your emotions so you can get on with the business of crying, laughing, being angry—your goal is to do what it takes to uncover and release your old hurts and free yourself!

4. **Take a bubble bath** and put candles and photos of your loved one in the room. You can reminisce about what you miss, maybe tell her something that needs to be said, or ask for help. Try dunking your head under the water and blowing bubbles to break up the mood, and even pray to feel levity again.

5. **Blast his favorite music and dance!** Or sit still and listen, and let your emotions roll.

6. **Make an appointment** to speak with your loved one on the other side. Show up and start talking! Talk until there's nothing left to say. Tell him everything. Are you angry with him? Do the two of you have unfinished business? Talk and talk some more! He's listening, and I have confidence he will respond in some fashion. Even if it's just through your own mind, a simple sign, or a renewed sense of peace. There is no downside.

7. **Grab your journal for the Remember You exercise.** Remind yourself of *your* wonderful talents, gifts, skills, abilities, blessings, and the other people in the world who love you. Write everything down in your journal and carry

it with you as a way to remind yourself of what's within and all around you. Take care of yourself by leaning on the support of your loved ones here on earth. Living Angels are here to help you through the void. Be open to their blessings.

8. **Write up a Loved-One Impact List**—an account of the positives and negatives this person brought into your life, both here on earth and from the Great Beyond. How did this person change your life for the better, help you break out of your shell, open you up emotionally? What were the gifts of your relationship? In realizing the positive impact she had on your life, don't be surprised if you see that she accomplished just what she needed to do in order to help you move forward. Trust that she can continue to serve you, only in a different capacity.

9. **Make your What I Like Best List.** Grieving can be overwhelming. It's easy to get stressed and see everything as routine, monotonous, and devoid of meaning. You can forget what you like to do—what's fun and makes you happy. This exercise will remind you so that you can schedule moments for things that nurture you, whenever the time is right.

10. **Make your bucket list.** You still have the opportunity to live your dreams. Why not? Your loved one is now on the other side, cheering you on, giving you the confidence boost you'll need. So get creative and dream big.

11. **Celebrate!** As odd as it sounds, I encourage you to celebrate the happiness your loved one brought to your life. Celebrate your memories and the fact that you now have a beautiful Angel on the other side rooting for your every step! Someone who knows you and loves you unconditionally. Someone who understands the challenges and heartache of life on earth. Someone who can lend a hand when needed.

12. **Stop and breathe.** When you're in a state of grief and feel paralyzed, stop and ask yourself what you think your loved one would want you to do. Would she want you to abandon all hope and faith, to stop focusing on your talents,

goals, and blessings? Of course not! Write down in your journal what you think your loved one would ask you to do right now. Then do it. This is powerful—a real mood changer.

If none of the above exercises tickle your fancy, allow me to expand on one additional exercise that I believe should be part of your everyday life, no matter what experience you are faced with. It's called **Acceptance,** a key **Fundamental.**

The Fourth Fundamental: Acceptance

If you feel stuck where you are, caught in a cycle of negativity, or sorry for yourself, know that I've been there. The Acceptance exercise has been tremendously powerful for me, helping me change my vibe. It's simple, but not always easy—as it's all about accepting yourself, your life, your experiences, your challenges, your emotions, and yes, even accepting the fact that your loved one is no longer here in the physical sense. Acceptance requires you to let go of the control and the burning desire to change everything and anything to fit your vision. It's difficult to do the acceptance exercise, but when you gather the nerve to accept all things, you'll be amazed at the miracles that occur. Life is long (usually) and full of ups and downs (for sure), so why not accept and embrace it all?

So, instead of remaining in a boo-hoo kitty state, accept that things aren't exactly as you envisioned them. Accept life just as it is—the good, the bad, and the indifferent. The act of acceptance actually begins the movement of energy and ultimately allows everything to transform.

So how do you get started? Through acceptance statements. I voice my acceptance statements out loud, and I mean them when I say them, feeling my emotions as I go. I start every statement with "I accept the fact that . . ." and continue on. (See below examples, but also feel free to craft your own.) Say them whenever you want to—all day long, if you have to.

Here are a few to get you started:

- "I accept the fact that I am afraid of _____." (Make a statement for each of your fears.)
- "I accept the fact that everything I've gone through in life is what it is—I can't change the past, but I can learn and grow from it."
- "I accept the fact that I'm having a terrible day!"
- "I accept the fact that I have no idea what my future holds, and this scares the jeepers out of me!"
- "I accept the fact that my loved one is no longer here physically but is close by in spirit."
- "I accept the fact that I am so angry at _____."

These affirmations don't just help with grieving the loss of a loved one. They help ease my stress in many more common situations. For example, when my youngest son was born, my two-year-old son adjusted as best he could, but after six months, he decided he no longer wanted to take naps (even though he desperately needed them and became a monster without them). Each day I dreaded nap time. I was tense, stressed out, impatient. This went on for weeks. I was about to lose my mind until I remembered to take my own advice and accept the situation. I started saying, "I accept the fact that my son doesn't want to take naps, even though a nap reenergizes him and keeps him happy (and Mom, too)!"

As soon as I started accepting my reality (and no longer tried to control the outcome), he started conking out again for his naps. It was a breeze. I laughed, wishing I'd figured out the ease of surrender earlier.

———◆◆◆———

You may think all of these suggestions seem silly, time consuming, or not worth your energy, but I ask you to give them a shot. I believe you'll be amazed by the shifts in your being just by doing any one of these exercises. Sometimes healing is more about taking the time to do something that isn't part of your everyday routine. Mix it up and trust yourself.

Tips and Considerations for Grieving

Finally, as we go on to the next chapter, remember:

- You cannot heal until you feel! Feel your emotions and let 'er rip. Only then can you laugh with ease.
- There is no right or wrong way in which to grieve. Work through it in a way that feels natural to you.
- Ask for (and accept) help from others, including your spirit friends.
- Know that you (and everyone else) are on a unique time-line. Don't judge your process. Everything happens in divine timing.
- You don't have to show your strength to prove you're strong. The weak shall inherit the earth. You are strongest in your vulnerability.

$\Rightarrow$ 3 $\Leftarrow$

Rock Star Moments: Bigger than Life Signs

Now that you've got a grip on ramping up your faith and relieving your grief, I'd like to introduce you to the different ways in which people experience their loved ones on the other side. In this chapter, we're going to talk about the *big*, dramatic, awe-inspiring connections.

Dad Pulled Me Out of the Car

Racecar driver Dale Earnhardt Jr. was on the track at the Daytona 500 in 2001 when he witnessed in his rearview mirror the crash that instantly killed his father several hundred yards behind him. Just over three years later, in a road race in Sonoma, California, Dale Earnhardt Jr. was in a fiery crash that nearly took his own life.

"Do you think your dad was watching when you ran into trouble at Sonoma?" Mike Wallace of *60 Minutes* asked Dale Earnhardt Jr.

" . . . Absolutely. I don't know how else to put it . . . I don't have an explanation for it other than when I got into the infield care center I had my PR man by the collar, screaming at him to find the guy that pulled me out of the car."

"Nobody helped you get out," his PR man said.

"That's strange, because I swear somebody had me underneath my arms and was carrying me out of the car. I mean, I swear to God," replied Earnhardt.

"And that was your dad?" Wallace asked.

"Yeah, I don't know. You tell me," said Earnhardt. "It freaks me out today just talking about it. It just gives me chills."

<hr />

That's what I like to call a Rock Star moment! So was the time you read about in the introduction, when my sister Kathy appeared to me soon after her death. In Rock Star moments, our departed loved ones visit us in physical form or make themselves known through dreams, noises, or feelings that are so intense, so obvious, that you'd have to go out of your way to ignore them. These instances, which happen less frequently than the more common Subtle Signs, are *big*. Examples include:

- You're in danger and receive a heavenly warning or an actual helping hand that arrives just in time to save your life.
- You turn the corner of the hallway to see your loved one standing there, only to disappear seconds later.
- You wake up with a jolt in the middle of the night, knowing that your loved one has just been killed.
- Your loved one visits you in a dream with an important message, moves objects in front of you, or generally affects your environment with traces of his personality that leaves you with an undeniable sense that he's been there and wants you to know it.

No matter how or when a Rock Star moment occurs, you're left with a very real sense of peace and love (after any initial shock), and a rock-solid belief that life does indeed continue on after death. Often, the feelings in your mind and body are so remarkably profound that you cannot even remotely put them into words. In this chapter and throughout the pages of this book, you'll find many stories to help you recognize, understand, and invite your own Rock Star moments as well as moments of a subtler kind. No matter the form or place, all experiences validate the timeless beauty of love and our connections with our loved ones on the other side of the veil.

As for Rock Star moments, these bigger-than-life (or death!) moments can happen anytime—even years after a person passes. While they most often take place soon after someone dies, or during times of extreme grief or urgency (like the story below shared with me from Natalie Kottke of Los Angeles, California), keep your eyes and ears open—because you just never know!

Grammy Told Me to Turn Left

In Natalie's own words:
Praying to my Grammy is a staple in my life, even at the age of twenty-eight. I had never realized the power of this practice until I was faced with a potentially fatal moment.

Add 317 days of commuting to work in one year (that's 720 total hours logged, or 140 miles of rubber burned daily) to massive sleep deprivation and endless cups of joe, and you can imagine the walking disaster waiting to happen that I'd morphed into. My friends thought I was insane to drive this much for work. Did they not read the news of high unemployment? Ignoring them, I kept my eye on the road, certain that my case of premeditated insanity would soon be over once I moved closer to work. *Millions of Americans commute obscene hours each week.* Why should I expect to be any different?

On the 314th day, at eleven p.m. going about my drive as usual with windows foggy from the night's moist air, I cruised my way up the slick streets of Chino Hills, California, in my 2003 two-door Honda Civic. I was no stranger to this winding canyon. This night, however, came on the heels of an unusually long workday, making my youthful stamina less dependable. The roads were extra damp and my eyelids extra heavy. I sped slowly, sensing my body shutting down. I rolled down the windows, welcoming the cool breeze, and turned up the volume on Bob Dylan with my right hand, gripping the steering wheel tightly with my left.

With only a few moments to go until I reached home, my eyelids shut as I made my way up the top of a steep hill.

My head fell back as my car whipped out of control. Within a hair of a second, the airbags deployed, and I came to. In that moment, I heard a whisper: *Take the steering wheel and turn left. Hard!* Like a dog tweaking my head, ears perked, I heeded the voice. I obeyed.

Trying desperately to manipulate my hands over the deployed and smoking airbag, I found nothing but a stuck wheel. As hard as I tried, I couldn't get it to budge. As I struggled to control my car, I remembered that there was a three-foot-high island coming up ahead. *Turn left, hard,* I heard the voice say again. Once more, I placed my hands on the steering wheel. Time seemed to slow down. I prayed to my Grammy to help me. Gripping my hands and bearing down on the wheel one final time, I made a hard left. This time, the steering wheel turned with ease.

Call it what you will—the power of prayer, a sign being whispered in my ear at the right moment, or plain old instincts—I don't know. What I do know is that the steering wheel didn't budge the first time I tried, and had I not listened closely and turned left, I would have ended up dead center in the middle of the island with much more trouble to deal with than deployed airbags.

Natalie's Rock Star moment could also be called divine intervention. No matter the label, this example shows the power loved ones have to intervene on our behalf when their assistance doesn't otherwise interfere with a life lesson we need to learn. In Natalie's case, her grandmother's action probably saved her life. She could have chosen to ignore the instruction she received that night; she, like all of us, has the power of choice. But thankfully, the stronger the voices, feelings, or signs, the more likely we are to take immediate action.

I call this **Angel on Your Shoulder:** You're in urgent danger, whether you know it or not. Your loved one, from a higher vantage point, reaches out to steer you in the right direction—often to your amazement.

Think back on your life. Have you ever come close to being in an accident? Maybe you were about to run a yellow light, but at the last second, you heard, *"Stop!"* or felt an urgent need to hit the brakes. Just as you came to a screeching halt, your heart sank as you watched a car speed through a solid red light in the lane you would have crossed over had you gone forward. Perhaps you've witnessed a crash. Or maybe you've experienced a near miss when something froze you to the curb just as a bus or truck swooshed by inches from where you stood. These, too, can be Rock Star moments, even if you didn't realize them at the time. My guess is that a loved one, a Guardian Angel with a power greater than you can imagine, stepped in on your behalf at just the right moment to ensure that all would be well.

———◆———

There are many situations that instigate heavenly support or communication. These include:

- **Ask and You Shall Receive:** You're making a conscious, heartfelt plea or prayer—calling out for specific information, guidance, help, literally pulling them in.
- **Holy Confirmation:** You're in great emotional pain, and a visitation or radical sign from your loved one offers the peace and comfort you need at this important time.
- **You Complete Me:** The person who has passed away has left behind unfinished business and wants you to have information that will take care of something, either for you, her, or someone else.
- **Instant Connection:** Love conquers all. The indelible bond you have with this person crossing over (or the love you have for him) pierces through time and space and alerts you to the moment of his departure.
- **Two as One:** Your loved one temporarily visits you to the point of physically taking over your body. While this differs

from living for two—in which you decide to expand your life to have more meaning by doing the things your dear departed either loved to do or always wanted to do—this experience is far more rare . . . a true Rock Star event.

- **Lighten Up:** Pranksters come in all shapes and sizes, even ones no longer with us. Ever hear the saying *Once a joker, always a* joker? Apparently one's sense of humor is never lost. . . .

You've already read examples of these (and more), and will continue to. The important thing I want you to remember is that your experiences are yours and are perfect in their own right. While I hope you use the many examples in this book as a guide to inspire you and help open up your mind and heart, my greatest wish is that you steer clear of comparing your experiences to anyone else's. There is no right or wrong way to communicate with the other side. In fact, all is as it should be.

◦ ◆ ◦

While I like to think of Rock Star moments as a personal Big Bang, I don't want you to despair if you've never experienced one. Some people never do, and that's okay. You can still communicate with your loved one! In the next chapter, we'll look at the more Subtle Signs that reveal their presence. All you need to do is pay close attention and you'll come to recognize those subtler signs more and more.

People universally experience many of the same things—both large and small—when it comes to the messages they receive following the death of a loved one. The subtler communications can feel so common or brief or unusual that they're easily dismissed as coincidence, imagination, even paranoia. The ways in which your loved one could already be reaching out may surprise (and delight) you.

I'll soon walk you through the easy steps to create a two-way relationship through the smallest of whispers, sensations, and coincidences. And you'll become your own investigative Angel journalist, recording these signs in your **Angel-in-a-Pocket Journal.** But for now, let's look more deeply into the big, bold signs. Because no matter how they present themselves, Rock Star moments are heightened experiences that leave an impact. Sometimes, too, as you're about to see, Rock Star moments are more playful, even a bit absurd. Like the way in which the eldest Tisch daughter of Los Altos, California, used to deal with the ghost in their house—the perfect "Lighten up" story.

The Prankster Poltergeist Who Watched Out for Linda

"**Growing up, I used to joke with an old lady ghost** I'd see in our living room," said Linda. "It started with her turning off the lights from time to time. I'd see her in quick flashes, and laugh, telling her to turn the lights back on. She always did. Then, she'd do the same with the stereo. It was the strangest thing. But I never felt afraid. One day I told my mother what she looked like—short, plump, white hair and glasses. Sure enough, a neighbor revealed that the original owner of the house looked just like her! I always felt that this heavenly kind of grandma was looking out for us, like an older Guardian Angel."

<hr>

I categorize this next story as a **Holy Confirmation** Rock Star intervention—additional proof to me that our loved ones can indeed reach out and provide us comfort, often gifting us with a form of instant healing from grief or pain.

Anne's Mother Climbs under the Covers

Anne and Lou had been married fifty years and had a very close relationship. They had survived many ups and downs, including their own tough childhoods, the Great Depression, and the separation of World War II, when Anne raised their two daughters alone for a few years while Lou fought alongside his four brothers.

Later on in life, with their children grown, Anne lost her mother to natural causes. Her passing filled Anne with grief, guilt, and depression, and she found it impossible to let go. Anne was still haunted by the childhood memories of seeing her mother abused by her father. She had so admired her mother's strength and the tough but tender unconditional love her mother had shown her throughout the years. In her grief, she relived over and over the secrets they created and shared so the two of them, along with her siblings, would be safe from her father. As often happens after death, Anne didn't know if she could go on living. After experiencing depression for several months, one cold night while Anne and Lou were sleeping, Anne was awoken by cold air. The blankets of their bed were lifted up by someone climbing into bed.

"Hurry up and get into bed; it's cold," Anne said to Lou.

"What? I was just going to say the same thing to you," he said.

Terrified, they realized someone else was climbing into bed with them, but they couldn't see anyone. As the covers fell back down to cover them, Anne felt a very heavy weight upon her entire body.

"Oh God, what is this? Who is this?" she said. Anne was unable to move with the force holding her down. Then Anne saw her. Her mother was lying right on top of her, face to face. Her mother smiled and began brushing her hair with her hand, and caressing her face.

"The feeling I had was of an overwhelming peaceful calm," Anne told me. "It was beautiful and enveloped my whole body." Anne's fear quickly disappeared, although her heart was beating so fast she was surprised she didn't have a heart attack. Lou just lay there with his eyes bulging out in complete amazement, as he could also see his mother-in-law.

Anne called out, "Mom!" and at that moment, the silhouette of her mother lifted off of her, drifted down the bed, and flew right through the wall of their bedroom. Anne and Lou sat quietly for several minutes, staring at the wall, wondering what had just happened. They both realized the blessing they had just received, and Anne was finally at peace with herself and her past.

"There was so much love and peace that surrounded me when my mother visited," she said. "I had no doubt my mother visited so that I could let go of the guilt and anger I felt, and truly live life to the fullest. I am so thankful."

It's stories like these that help us know that our loved ones care deeply that we move forward in our lives, letting go of guilt, shame, and any other emotions holding us back. Hanging on to our loved ones in an unhealthy way, or focusing on those things we cannot change only freezes us in place. This is not what they want for us. Think about it: if the tables were reversed, and you were the one who transitioned first, what would you want for your loved ones?

◆

This next example may sound playful, but I assure you that it most definitely did not *feel* playful at the time. I categorize this story as an **Ask and You Shall Receive** Rock Star moment in that I was making a conscious, heartfelt plea or prayer—calling out for specific help, literally pulling in support.

Kathy Clears the Weather

Six months pregnant with my first son, I flew with my mom and aunt to a relative's wedding in Austin, Texas. A connecting flight through Dallas on the return trip was grounded due to severe thunderstorms flooding parts of Texas, affecting various airports.

They said it was temporary. We weren't worried; we'd already boarded the plane and were on the tarmac. An hour went by with no movement. Then another thirty minutes without word. My legs tightened up, yet we continued to sit for another hour. I had packed lots of food, but with hormones raging, my body ached. The baby was kicking, I felt claustrophobic, and my emotions were rolling out of control. I wanted *out! Now!*

The pilot came on over the loudspeaker. "Ladies and gentlemen, I'm sorry to inform you, but it looks like this flight will most likely be canceled." I couldn't handle the thought of de-boarding, schlepping to find our luggage, and driving around an unfamiliar city trying to locate a place to stay. I was incredibly uncomfortable; I just wanted to sleep in my own bed. Sick to my stomach, I started sobbing.

Then it hit me. I knew exactly what to do. I couldn't believe I'd forgotten the easiest, most powerful tool I have access to anytime, anywhere . . . prayer! I looked out the window and prayed to my sister: *Please, Kath, clear the weather so we can get home tonight. I can't take this anymore. Please?! I need to go home!*

I turned to my aunt to ask her for a tissue and looked down at the book she was reading. She was on page 310—the number 310 leaped out at me, popping off the page like I was watching a 3-D movie. (Once again, Kathy was letting me know she was nearby and taking care of things by bringing that number right up into my face. I've only recently learned that it's also one of the main area codes of Los Angeles, the City of Angels!) I felt a warmth envelop me as if I had suddenly snuggled into a heavy fur coat, and I knew that I would indeed sleep in my own bed that night. Instead of asking my aunt for that tissue, I said: "We *will* be flying home tonight!" She chuckled, since the captain had just announced otherwise, shook her head, and said, "I hope so, honey."

The captain came over the loud speaker not a minute later, this time to say: "Well, folks, I'm shocked to be saying this, but we have just been cleared for takeoff." Everyone on the plane cheered and clapped in complete amazement. Me? I got goose bumps all over my body, looked up to the sky, and blew a kiss to my sister. No matter how many times she appears to come to my aid, answer my prayers, or galvanize the Heavenly Host, no matter how commonplace these miracles have become in my life, they still never cease to amaze me.

You just never know when your loved one may be available to lend a hand, or even clear the weather! Have faith and believe in the power of your sacred, spiritual connection.

━━━◆◆◆━━━

While the last two stories were a bit out of the norm, the next two stories are nearly unbelievable in their uniqueness (but that's what makes them so memorable)! If I didn't interview these clients myself, I'd have a tough time believing them as well.

A Phone Call from John and Mom

Zen lost her mother to what appeared to be a suicide in 1993 (which, years later, was found to be a chemical reaction between two medicines). Her younger brother, John, died in a freak accident a few years later when a landslide in the mountains cut him off from civilization. He was thirty-three years old. Trapped, he ultimately died of dehydration.

Zen was devastated by these two tragic deaths. Then, one day in 2007, her eccentric friend Molly, who happened to be a psychic, came for a visit and kept telling Zen she had a message for her but couldn't remember what it was. Finally, while heading down the stairs to leave two hours later, Molly turned around and said, "Oh! I remember what it was. You have to call your mom!"

"Oh, honey, my mom is dead," Zen said.

"I know she is, but on Mother's Day I want you to sit on your couch, hold a phone up to your ear, and pretend to call her. Then, just wait."

Yeah, sure, thought Zen as she closed her door. She forgot all about the bizarre recommendation, but when Mother's Day rolled around and another friend made an unexpected visit with a beautiful arrangement of fresh flowers, it jogged her memory. After a nice visit, Zen placed the flowers in a vase, sat down on her couch, and picked up her cordless phone, just as Molly had said to do three weeks prior. With zero expectations, she thought, *I'm just going to do this.*

Zen went through the motion of dialing the phone number her mom used to have, and then she heard the phone actually ring! Next she heard her mother's voice answer the phone.

"Hello!" said a woman. Zen assumed the voice of her mother had to be in her head.

"Hi, Mom, how are you doing?" Zen asked.

"Oh, I'm doing good," responded her mom.

"Are you happy?" Zen asked curiously.

"Oh yes, very much so."

And then Zen asked, "How's John?"

"He's doing great! He's right here. Talk to him." She handed the phone to Zen's brother.

The idea of talking with John had never crossed Zen's mind; this was all a lark—she was merely following instructions. When John's voice hit the phone, she couldn't believe her ears and froze in place. Numb, but very much aware, Zen listened to each word in awe.

Zen's nickname as a kid was Ferfer.

"Hey, Ferfer! How ya doing?" he asked. He followed that up with a long thirty-minute monologue of how proud he was of her, listing the things he'd seen her doing, recognizing her accomplishments with great care. Tears poured down Zen's face as she sat and listened. He encouraged her to keep up the great work, and then he handed the phone back to Mom.

In an exasperated voice, her mom said, "Well . . . your brother pretty much said it all!" Zen laughed. That was just what her mother would have said while living, which gave Zen the added confidence that she was indeed speaking with her beloved mother.

"Well, I don't have anything else to say," her mother continued. "John said it all. But, I love you!"

Zen and her mom said their goodbyes and hung up. As she sat on the couch and let this all sink in, all that she could think was, *Wow! I was expecting a simple, ridiculous, pretend conversation.*

Zen is still shocked by the quality time she was able to share with her mother and brother. Those healing conversations were just what she needed to keep the faith in herself and in life.

You don't have to pick up the phone and pretend to have a conversation with anyone. You can simply talk out loud in private or write a letter. Your loved ones are only a thought away—as close as your heart. It's not the form that matters, but your intention that makes a connection.

Body Double at Burning Man

Sometimes, two different Rock Star events converge to make for a truly shocking experience. In this instance, Sheri decided to experiment with **living for two** (which you'll learn about in Chapter 7), but also ended up in a **two-as-one** situation. Let me explain.

Sheri lost her younger brother when he was in his late twenties. Before he died, he frequently spoke of wanting to attend Burning Man with her, her favorite annual summer trek to the Nevada desert where tens of thousands of people get together and build their own self-reliant universe for a week-long experiment in a temporary community. As the name implies, the event includes the burning of an effigy—a massive statue of a wooden man.

The year after her brother passed, Sheri made her usual pilgrimage to Burning Man and ventured out to sit beyond all of the people, out on her own. As she looked back at the picturesque scene, she began to cry. She'd always wanted her brother to experience the eccentric atmosphere that supported being who you want and finding a way to give to others, and she was overwhelmed with emotions at the thought of not being able to experience anything with her brother ever again. Then it dawned on her. *Wait a minute. Why can't I invite him to be here with me now? Why can't he come with me as I make my way through the events?*

So she did just that. Sheri simply asked her brother to join her and to let her know when he got there—to somehow make her aware of how he felt. Suddenly, out of nowhere, Sheri felt him. She smelled his familiar scent. She heard his voice.

"I'm here," he said. Then, to her shock, he ever so gently settled into her body. For seven hours, Sheri still felt like herself, but she swears that her brother was happily controlling her body.

"It's as if he'd asked me to move over while he drove," she laughed. "He was having so much fun! I've never danced like that before in my life. One of the most poignant memories for me was the feeling that he had no worries about what we looked like, or what other people thought. Nothing mattered except being fully alive and having the most fun imaginable."

That night Sheri experienced things she'd never desired to do before.

"I know my brother was living out his dreams through my body," she said. "I mean, come on. I'd never intentionally break dance, pull wheelies on a bicycle (like my brother always did), or act like a crazy guy, except, of course, that night. It gave me such a new respect for being alive, for understanding that life is so precious and to live fully every day."

Kathy has never, to my knowledge, taken over my physical body. But I have, as you'll soon see, imagined that she was with me when doing adventurous things she loved. Again, whatever feels right for you is what's right for you. I will advise, though, to do your best to be open-minded regarding how your loved ones may reveal themselves to you. While you may never have an experience as out there as those in the last two stories, the possibilities are endless, and I don't want you to miss out because of fear or limiting beliefs. Trust yourself, your loved ones, and life. I sincerely believe the rest will take care of itself.

People ask me if it's possible they've experienced a Rock Star moment without noticing it. Yes. When I saw my sister in my bedroom soon after she'd passed, the event jump-started our initial communication, but I suppose I *could* have missed her, or talked myself out of what I'd seen. Maybe something similar has happened to you, and you weren't sure if it was real so you second-guessed your experience. I've had clients, not unlike me that night

I jumped under my covers, who also panicked in the moment they experienced a big bang connection, and then worried incessantly that they blew their big moment—as if their window of communication had closed forever. I assure you, that's not the case. You can start to reconnect at any time and invite your loved ones into your world. They've entered another world, and they may be waiting for an invitation back into yours (just like the story of Zen and her phone conversation with her mother and brother). As you trust the process, your communication will flourish.

Some of the most comforting, bizarre, and dramatic of the Rock Star moments happen in our dreams. I call these dreams **Sleep Signs,** and they can be so powerful that you're going to want to pay attention. In fact, I tell all my clients (and that includes you!) to keep a pen and paper handy by the bed because once you start paying attention, and once your angelic loved ones know your sleepy eyes and ears are open, it can get downright busy at night!

Visited in Dreams

Has it ever dawned on you that you spend a third (or more) of your life *asleep?*

Unless you're a workaholic (not you, of course) you spend a lot of time semiconscious. But what if you're not as unaware as you think? What if you could use this valuable time to receive heavenly messages and help navigate your life? What if you could receive invaluable guidance from your dreams?

This is nothing new.

Recorded tablets show that primitive peoples have interpreted their dreams as far back as 4000 BC. All humans, even animals, dream every night. The point is: this is an ideal place to establish a connection with your loved one, allowing your dreams to guide you.

Why not start tonight?

In paying attention to your dreams, problems can be solved, questions answered, new visions inspired, and signs revealed. I have a client who works on her laptop for a living, and in three separate dreams over ten years, she saw her laptop smoking and then dying.

Each time, she'd wake up, and her hard drive would crash and the computer would die that day—one time it literally started smoking! While this dream became helpful over time, as she finally learned to back up her data immediately upon waking up in those instances, some dreams warn us about life and death, literally.

Linda and Carol's mother had died from liver cancer five years prior. One morning Carol called Linda after a vivid dream. Having only seen their mother in a dream once before, she knew this one was important.

In the dream, their mother pushed a shopping cart right up to Carol in the supermarket aisle, looking her squarely in the eyes. "Move home on October 31," she said.

Later in the dream, her mother called her over the phone and again said: "Move home October 31." The dream ended with Carol moving home and Linda arriving soon afterward, luggage in tow. Carol woke up, called her sister and said, "What do you think this means?"

The sisters lived in Southern California and their father in Northern California. They were all used to the earth dancing, thus, Linda figured the warning referred to a coming quake, which might necessitate them moving away to live with their father. When October 31 came and went without so much as a tremor, the sisters assumed that the dream hadn't meant what they thought it had. The following year, however, on October 30, their father called to say that he had stage 4 cancer and needed surgery that week. Carol moved home the next day, October 31. Linda followed days later. They took turns living with him full time over the next eighteen months, and both girls were present when he passed away.

I've been told that some psychics believe it takes an enormous amount of energy for somebody who has passed away to visit us physically, to make their voice heard audibly, or to send a very specific message to us through dreams. If a loved one comes to you in a dream, with a specific message—especially if she's looking you in the eyes or calling you on a phone—pay special attention because what she's saying is *important*. Although Carol's dream was a year off, it still held true. Had she and her sister not listened, perhaps they wouldn't have moved home so quickly and would have missed invaluable time with their beloved father. "That time was some of the best of our lives," the women told me. "We're so grateful Mom took the time and energy to give us the warning."

What I find most magical about dreams is their ability to cut through time and space to show us what's really going on behind the scenes. If you've seen Harry Potter use his invisibility cloak, you know what I'm talking about.

As you'll see in this next story, sometimes messages from our loved ones appear on the surface as negative, or they don't initially provide the warm fuzzy you'd hope for. Once again, it's about being open-minded and trusting that all experiences, all situations, all messages and signs are gifts waiting to be discovered.

Grandma's Got Your Back!

Karen had a close relationship with her grandmother who passed away over thirty-five years ago. Growing up, she often felt even closer with her gram than with her own mother, so it was no surprise to her when she'd sense her gram around her, especially during challenging times. One in particular related to her profession and a specific woman with which she worked. Karen is a hard-working, successful businesswoman who is well-respected for her accomplishments. For many years she worked for a Fortune 500 company, running a significant portion of the business. A new woman was hired to run another area of the business that was tightly tied to Karen's, requiring they work closely together.

"I felt like I was working in hell," Karen said. "This other woman just seemed to be out to get me, and she did everything she could to make me look bad and cause me grief. It was working." At night Karen would leave work—the job she once loved—and dread going back the next morning. Day in and day out was spent worrying about what this woman was doing, fearing what was next, and contemplating leaving. The stress consumed her and was making her sick—until her gram intervened through a revealing dream.

In the dream, Karen went to visit her gram at the house she lived in over thirty-five years ago when she was alive. The room was the same, except for the colors, or lack of them. Gram's kitchen was once painted a colorful apricot, with green tile and a vivid red, old-fashioned table and chairs. But in the dream, when Karen walked into her Gram's kitchen, the walls, tile, ceiling, and floor were all white. The only color in the room was red—the table and chairs. What made this feel especially disturbing was that bright red was also splattered all over the walls, like blood. Karen didn't see her gram, but she heard her welcome her into the kitchen. Karen stood there, feeling the fear coursing through her.

"Why is there blood all around?" she asked her grandmother.

"Look in the other room," she heard.

The kitchen opened up to Gram's dining room. Karen reluctantly turned around to look. It was dark, but she could see clearly who was standing there—the woman who had been causing her grief at work! She held a knife in her hand, with blood dripping from the blade. Behind this woman stood the executive who oversaw both women. He had an evil smile on his face and was laughing under his breath. Karen couldn't speak.

"Now you know," her gram said.

When Karen woke up, she was disturbed by the gory images in this dream. But when she took a moment to digest and process the deeper message from her grandmother, she knew exactly what she needed to do—quit her job! Within a few weeks, she resigned from the company and moved on to a much better job. Karen has had other dreams in her life involving blood and the color red, and she has learned that rather than fear these dreams, she needs to pay attention to the message and the guidance being provided. This is one symbol she's been given that protects her.

Had her gram not sent this timely message, Karen probably would have continued work in misery as she was stabbed in the back.

⋙◆⋘

What did you dream about last night? Last week? Last month? Take a moment and jot down what you remember each morning in your Angel Journal. Feel free to ask pointed questions, writing them down before you fall asleep, and see what messages you receive throughout the night. If your dreams seem fuzzy, stick with this practice. They will get clearer. You will start to understand their symbolism. It's as if your unconscious knows you're finally paying attention and it starts speaking to you in a more obvious language. I always try to go with the feeling of a dream. For instance, if I ask for a specific answer about something and I wake up feeling badly, I know the answer is probably no. If, on the other hand, I ask a question, have a good dream, and wake up feeling terrific, I often interpret this to be a yes.

The method is to filter this all through your intuition (or your heart) and listen to that still, small voice inside of you.

Feeling Is Believing

Jill was a new author and had just released her first book. She didn't have much money with which to publicize her literary baby, and she was frustrated that she couldn't hire a publicist. One day out of the blue, a publicist called her from New York. She had read the book, loved it, and wanted to help Jill get publicity. But the woman wanted to be paid a fee Jill couldn't afford. Jill prayed to her mother, who had recently passed. *What will happen if I hire this woman to help me?*

Jill's dream that night was unlike anything she'd ever experienced. In it, she and her husband were on a cruise ship, dancing and laughing and playing with money. When she woke up, Jill was confused. She believed the dream was telling her that she had good fortune coming and should hire this woman, but something about doing so just felt off. Not only could she not afford the fee without great sacrifice, but her gut feeling was that it wasn't time. So, she prayed for another option.

Within a week, a friend called and gave Jill and her husband a ten-day, all-expenses-paid trip to the Caribbean on a cruise ship! "You two have had too much stress lately and never had a proper honeymoon," she said. "And I want to change that."

Jill and her husband took the cruise and had a blast. They rekindled their romance and came home happier than they'd been in years. The kicker? While Jill was floating around the Atlantic, her book was covered on multiple news networks all on its own, and it sold out in stores nationwide.

Sweet dreams. Zzzzz . . .

———◆——

Sometimes it's best to let go and trust, allowing things to happen on their own, in divine time and divine order. We, as humans, have a tendency to want to control everything, to figure out the how and why and what, even when it's not ours to yet know. It was healing for Jill to receive such a fabulous gift of an all-expenses-paid trip. And it was even more of a blessing to reconnect with her husband away from work and stress for the first time in years while allowing the Universe to work for her and her book.

I encourage you to try this in your own life. Pray. Ask for guidance, signs, and messages, and then let it all go and allow things to unfold beautifully before your eyes, just when the time is right.

Don't Slow Your Roll!

Many people get frustrated waiting for a Rock Star sign to appear (or reappear) and miss the beautiful, little, Subtle Signs all around. That's what happened to my client Paula.

Paula had experienced several Rock Star moments—and she wanted more! The first came after crying for hours and feeling sorry for herself after losing her lover, Charlie, to cancer. A light bulb blew above her head just after she'd asked him for a sign to show her he was nearby. The second one came on a gloomy day after she'd gained a lot of weight drowning her sorrows in ice cream and junk food. She heard his voice tell her to get up and move and go for a walk, and that she would see a feather to let her know he was with her. After walking for a while without seeing anything, she was about to turn around when she felt nudged to go farther. As she approached the parked car up ahead, she saw a picture on the dashboard covered in feathers.

Paula said she got greedy. "I wanted more and more, and I felt dependent on the big show of support. When I didn't get it, I'd fall into depression and emotional chaos."

The Fifth Fundamental: Expectations

Considering Paula's situation, I worked with her on the **Fundamental of Expectations**. Paula was getting tripped up because she was losing faith in the process of life and her ability to connect with the other side, she had forgotten that she could reach out and make subtler connections, and she had unrealistic expectations about how things should occur. As we worked on releasing her expectations, knowing her connections would happen one way or another, she was more open to allowing events to unfold just as they were supposed to. Our minds and egos try to control all of our outcomes, just as they did with Paula. I reminded Paula that only the Divine knows.

As Paula worked with the subtler energies, she learned to release her stress and allow the magic to happen. She still holds out for Rock Star moments—don't we all? But she's also very much enjoying the beauty and subtle power of the little things.

Tips and Considerations for Finding Your Rock Star Moment

In closing, I'd like to leave you with a few tips and considerations as you reach out to your loved ones on the other side.

- It's important to remember that you can't control when or how your loved one will send you messages or signs.
- You can't control how many times you'll experience big moments of connection. And, in truth, this is not for you to decide.
- You *can* control your faith, your actions, and your expectations.
- Release those expectations (of your loved one coming to you in a dream, appearing to you in person, walking through your door) and free yourself (and your loved one) to whatever wants to happen, whether that be Rock Star status or sweet Subtle Signs.
- Most of all, remember that it's easy to get so hung up waiting for the big visitation or dream that you miss countless communications that do come in. Don't miss out! Have only one expectation: that you *will* receive messages and signs, divinely timed.

≈ 4 ≈

Subtle Signs: The Moments You Can Easily Miss

A re you paying attention? Did you see that? Can you feel that? Your loved one who has passed away may want to connect with you, to open your eyes, or nudge you toward something you might need or desire. The results can alter your course in the most positive of ways.

While the big signs can be hard to miss—especially when your loved one makes a grand entrance and appears out of nowhere, as Kathy did for me—the day-to-day Subtle Signs are often mistaken for merely happenstance or good luck. But you won't make that mistake after reading this chapter. No. You'll be trained to be on the lookout to stay alert so you don't miss a thing. I have no doubt you'll be comforted seeing just how plentiful and dependable these quieter, simpler, more everyday signs are, and how richly rewarding their many gifts can be.

You may feel a familiar touch while writing, taking your morning walk, or playing a piece of music. You may hear a whispered voice out of nowhere. Or you may simply experience a knowingness.

Wait. Watch. Listen. And marvel as the beauty unfolds.

Julie was cooking dinner, and as the potatoes came to a boil, she felt something urging her to pay attention. With the perfect timing—just before the lid popped—she turned down the heat, saving herself a mess to clean up. Mary just knew she was being guided to move to Arizona, hearing whisperings to that effect. Months after relocating, she landed a fantastic new job, had established meaningful friendships, and felt as if she'd come home. Both women had family members who had recently died and found themselves receiving more gut feelings and noticeable chance happenings than usual. Coincidence? Hmm.

A familiar fragrance might waft through the air. A quick vision or an intuitive hit may surface and leave you with a lingering sensation or a feeling about how to proceed. A heart-shaped balloon may float by during a vulnerable or lonely moment when your loved one seems to offer support. (This actually happened to a client of mine—when on her birthday, a Happy Birthday balloon flew over her house just after her mother died, one hundred miles from the nearest mid-sized town!) You may feel the sudden spark of static electricity as the hairs on your arms stand up, seeming to signal that someone's nearby or sending you a message. Butterflies, birds, floating feathers or flowers, phone calls, doorbells, and a thousand other well-timed occurrences may fly or flap or float or ring or buzz just when you need guidance. Be open to the phenomenon.

Slow down. Walk softer. Listen clearer.

Perhaps you've already noticed an increase in these heavenly messages in your life since your loved one passed away. Maybe you find yourself driving in your car, thinking about a decision you need to make or a question you have, and you get the answer through a message on the radio, a sign, or a knowingness. These perfectly timed answers help me move forward just when I need them.

The smaller, yet more frequent signs are the most obvious. The ones I know to look for. I like to call them my **Very Important Angel signs,** or my VIAs. They boost my confidence and reassure me. Still, it's easy to go through the day without recognizing these sweet signs that could be as small as a flower or as innocent as a hummingbird. (Sometimes, as if to get my attention, they'll be obvious like lightning.) Sure, you don't *need* signs in order to make decisions, but isn't it refreshing to know you have this spiritual support?

As you might guess, my sister Kathy's favorite number, 310, our code, is one of my VIAs. Another VIA sign I often receive is her favorite song, "Don't Stop Believin'," by Journey. She lets me know she's nearby when, as if by magic, the band serenades me through the airwaves.

Perhaps you have your own VIAs whirling all around you. Pay attention to those times when something out of the ordinary occurs and you automatically label it as a coincidence. Capture these moments in your journal. Here's how . . .

Angel in a Pocket

As we've discussed, you can ask for and encourage deeper communication with the beyond by using a journal to keep track of it all. Don't worry about capturing every little thing in writing if you don't want to. Find your pace. You don't want to become so obsessed with keeping track that you lose the fun of it. But you'll be amazed at the increased confidence you feel while forging this new two-way communication.

I can't say for certain if keeping a daily log increases the frequency of the miracles or if it just makes me more aware. Perhaps it's a little of both. But, either way, I encourage you to jot down whatever feels relevant—the moments during the day that either *feel* like they could be signs or definitely are. There's no right way to track them. If you happen to notice a color in the sky that's out of the ordinary, log it. (A friend of mine was praying to her deceased mother one evening and woke up in the middle of the night to see the sky lit up with what she says were fluorescent greens and yellows and blues around the full moon!) If you hear a specific lyric that speaks to you, jot it down. If you smell a familiar scent, note it. We often have a "knowing" before a revelation. Tracking these signs may reveal a greater purpose later or uncover a playful pattern your loved one is using to reach out to you.

Your Angel notepad can be whatever pocket journal you feel comfortable carrying around. It can be a cheapie, dime-store version; an ornate, luxurious, one-of-a-kind book; or an inscribed journal. Whatever's accessible to fish out when you *feel* or *see* something noteworthy. The point is that it will aid you in accessing invisible realms and will connect you with your loved one. And, not unlike jotting your dreams down—as we discussed in the previous chapter—I think greater results can present themselves by declaring in this way that you're paying attention and have the structure for allowing it to happen. Keep in mind; your insights may come at lightning speed in this beautiful dance, or at a tortoise's pace. But get ready to smile! Subtle signs pile up swiftly.

I love using my Angel Journal to keep track of the pivotal dates in my life and the things that happen on those heightened days. I call this **Angel Mapping.** For example . . .

More Than a Feeling

When I was first married, my husband and I decided that we were content with just us and we didn't want children. So when I was jolted out of my sleep at 3:10 a.m. one Sunday morning with a crystal-clear message: "You're supposed to have kids, *now*," I was worried my husband would think I'd lost my mind.

From the start, our timing seemed auspicious. We found out that I was pregnant on the twentieth anniversary of my sister's death. We made a doctor's appointment and learned that our due date for our son's arrival was my sister's birthday, November 8. In labor at the hospital, in room #8, we met our nurse. Her name? Kathy!

After our son Evan's first year, we decided to try for a second child. Just like the first time, we had some difficulties getting pregnant and opted for intrauterine insemination (IUI). This type of fertility method can't be timed; you simply go by the plan that's determined after each blood draw. Biology picked the dates, and nature complied only after our third insemination. As if by divine intervention—and I'm not making this stuff up—we got pregnant on November 8. Again, Kathy's birthday!

Had we not been **Angel Mapping**—recording these "coincidences," it could have been easy to overlook them or chalk them up to luck or happenstance. But your Angel Journal gives you perspective, revealing all the evidence you need to start seeing the magic. By logging these happenings, appointments, dates, and the like, you'll start to see a marked increase in both your awareness of and help from your personal Angels all around.

Before we journey farther into the subtler side of signs, I want to give you a few things to focus on as you start deepening your two-way connection.

Practice Being Alive in Your Body

Your five senses hold the key to expanding your awareness in the subtler world. As you practice being *in* your body, you'll start thinking like the Angel investigator you are. Let your senses be your guide.

1. **Sight.** Keep an eye out for visuals that appear out of nowhere or seem to be calling your attention. Things glowing, shimmering, vibrating, moving. Be open. Signs leave clues. When I go to an event, for instance, I will stop at the entrance of the room and check in with Kathy, asking if there's anyone in particular I'm supposed to meet. Then I scan the room. It's uncanny how many times I've zeroed in on someone who ends up being either a great friend or a business connection—all because my intent is to be aware of my surroundings in a subtle, magical way.

2. **Hearing.** From the celestial spheres to the caw of a bird, any noticeable sound can signal guidance. A blaring siren when you're speaking or thinking of something in particular could be a warning. Thunder? Perhaps your personal exclamation point. The meow of a cat? Time to get out the tuna, or a confirmation? Go with your gut. Trust what you hear, even if it's your own voice within.

3. **Taste.** Notice tastes that whisk you back to another time and trigger memories or feelings—your childhood kitchen, your grandmother's split pea soup, or a familiar restaurant may be beckoning you. Savor the sign and ask yourself what that memory is trying to tell you. Perhaps there's someone

you need to contact on this side? Perhaps it's a memory you want to cherish from the past? The possibilities (and flavors) are endless.

4. **Touch/Feel.** A piece of velvet or a comfy blanket . . . the touch of an elder's hand . . . the slick lacquer of an antique table . . . may spark something in you. Sit with the sensation. Let it speak to you kinesthetically. I have an elderly neighbor who lives alone. I would see her from time to time in her yard, but I didn't often have time to stop and chat. One day she gave me a hug and held my hand. The touch of her skin reminded me of my grandmother. That moment immediately took me back to my childhood memories and the love I have for my gram. I think I needed the remembrance as much as my neighbor needed the connection. And I've felt more connected to my grandmother ever since.

5. **Smell.** Breathe in the intoxicating aromas around you, using scent to connect. Sweet, exotic, rich jasmine; fresh-cut grass; spring; a late-summer barbeque; or rain-soaked, fall leaves. Take it in to sense what it's telling you. Often our deceased loved ones will speak to us at fragrant times of the year, reminding us to slow down and smell the beauty of our lives and everything around us.

Your senses are infinitely powerful; not only for living your day-to-day life, but also for experiencing increased awareness of the spiritual world.

Ask and You Shall Receive!

I want you to play with this: The next time you'd like angelic confirmation or guidance for *anything*, ask for a sign. Then wait patiently, staying open and watchful. I'm willing to bet the answers are whirling around you. For instance . . .

One day I had a strong intuitive hit to write a book. The desire descended upon me out of nowhere and threw me for a loop because it was something I had never once considered or dreamed of. I mean, don't you have to be obsessed with the desire to create art your whole life in order to make it happen? Not to mention, be living in a hovel somewhere, starving?

Needing the confidence boost to take action, I went to bed that night asking Kathy for a specific sign. Unbelievably, I woke up the next morning to an email from a coach I know, with the subject header: You Should Write a Book—I'm Glad I Did! He went on to recommend a writing course taught by a woman named Linda Sivertsen. I'd never thought of taking a writing course before, but my interest was piqued to say the least! I literally sat laughing at my computer, with joy racing through my whole body.

"Okay," I said out loud. "If writing a book is truly my next step, I need to see three red birds on the same branch sitting next to each other." That evening, I tucked my son in and began reading him a children's story. There on the first page were three red birds perched on a branch.

While it might seem more obvious to find these birds on a real branch in the backyard, signs come in many forms. When you ask, be open to the answers. The power of asking for something specific and receiving it in any form shows that your Angels are listening and unbounded by time and space (maybe even that they have a good sense of humor). Those answers—first the email and then later that evening the book, both written forms of communication—couldn't have been a more fitting pair of signs to write, and they led to what you've got in your hands. (By the way, I had no idea what to write about, but I took Linda's book proposal course and then traveled to her mystical mountain writing retreat where, while talking about my sister, she not only "saw" this book before I did and outlined it for me—but she helped me sell it and is now my coauthor! The two of us talk, and mostly *listen* to Kathy regularly, through our intuition, dreams, and synchronicities, as we cocreate. Imagine that.)

So go ahead and start asking for signs or support concerning decisions you're waffling over, actions you're afraid of taking, or answers to questions that seem to have no answer. Ask! If you don't, who will? When you're patient, faithful, and open, the answers, signs, and guidance you need are often lightning fast in their delivery. And, in the rare occasion when you do not receive clear answers to your requests, trust that for some reason, you're not yet meant to know which road to take. It's hard to trust in these times—I know!—my guess is that in hindsight you'll easily see the value in waiting. Perhaps there was a lesson you needed to learn or you were being protected from something you thought you wanted but would have regretted (often, the better path is one we haven't considered). Or maybe you gained confidence through the positive experience of figuring it out on your own. In these instances, I continue to ask for guidance and stay open. But I also move on to other areas of my life, where my loved ones *are* able to intervene and provide the additional guidance I long for, knowing that everything else will turn out as it should.

Subtle Signs in Action

Ever wonder how you got the last free spot in the parking lot? The best seat in the café? Or who put that money in the parking meter right before you got there? Things that fall into place feel divinely guided, and they often are.

If you're like me, when you're late and rushing, you still attempt to squeeze in a last errand before picking up the kids. Some days I begin to panic, but I calm myself down and get the *feeling* that my sister Kathy is surrounding me. That's when I know there's a spot up ahead. Sure enough, a car leaves just as I get into position—I call this Rock Star parking. I record it in my journal so I can remember this later. Other auspicious happenings always seem to follow suit, like hitting every green light or getting the kids into the car one second before it starts pouring down rain.

This isn't luck, people. It's divine. I call these angelic gifts from above. I receive these blessings so often that I lose count when I don't track them. I've found, too, that taking time to review your log and say, "Thank you for everything," to my Angel friends renews my faith and energizes me. Not to mention, it keeps the blessings coming.

Now, regardless of wanting to be patient and find my own inner guidance, sometimes there's just no doubt that I need (and I use that term loosely) crystal-clear clarity about an issue. And,

I want it now! What then? That's when I ask for even more *specific* signs, even though my requests could seem to border on the insane.

The Lime-Green Truck

Recently, as I was running errands one morning, I asked to see a lime-green truck to confirm my decision to work part time. (A lime-green *anything* is an unusual request, especially on the highway. Because I felt desperate for a sign, I figured if I could see a hue I didn't think existed, that would be confirmation I could trust.) You see, I ached to take my boys out of day care so I could spend more of the week enjoying motherhood. I asked my request out loud. Twice. Moments later, I was shocked when a lime-green pickup truck appeared in front of me. *Thank you, Kathy!* That was all I needed.

I immediately had a conversation with my boss at IBM and asked to work part time. I was shocked when, in a bad economy and after extensive layoffs, my boss not only granted my request but also created a whole new job description to accommodate it! And I haven't seen a lime-green truck since.

What decisions are holding you back? Practice asking for specific signs—anything that comes to mind—and see what happens. You just might be amazed. Each successful outcome gives you confidence in further trusting life and your gut feelings. Case in point . . .

Lucky License Plate

Because my request for a sign about writing a book had turned out so well, I thought I'd do the same thing when faced with the issue of promoting this work. Every writer comes up against the daunting task of getting the word out. It's called building a platform and with 1,001 media outlets all clamoring for readers' attention, it's important to do what you can without expecting your publisher to do it all. I could write the most beautiful book about communicating with the other side, but if no one ever hears about it, all these messages would be hidden.

Not long ago I was presented with the idea of hosting my own radio show. I never thought of hosting a show before; in fact, I didn't have any desire to do so. But nonetheless, when something comes across my desk, I believe it's something I'm meant to address, or at the very least investigate. I did some research, and it seemed as though hosting a show to provide advice on a weekly basis to people who were grieving lost loved ones would be a win-win for everyone. I was worried, though, that I might not be able to carve out the time needed for this type of endeavor, with the kids and my job and my book deadline and all.

I did my typical request for help from my sister and the Divine. I asked them to please provide me with a sign that would let me know that hosting a radio show would be in my highest interest. That day, driving along the highway, I pulled in behind a car with the license plate "31GIFT." *Wow!* I thought. A voice popped into my ear that said, "There are gifts in taking this step."

For me, again, the number 310 or any iteration of it is always a sign from Kathy. I had no doubt that she was clearly sending me a message to move forward with the radio show and that there would be many gifts in the process.

I can tell you that after hosting my own show now for quite some time, the whole experience has been a treasure trove of blessings. There's the gift of connecting with people, the gift of helping others in need, the gift of friendship, the gift of giving and receiving, and the gift of an endless well of stories to share with you in your healing. It's been miraculous.

My point to you is this: be open to receiving messages and signs in all forms, and then listen to what your heart says is true for you. The license plate message itself was a strong sign for me, and so was the confirmation I heard in my ear at that very moment.

———•◆•———

Remember Paula from the previous chapter? The woman so focused on experiencing Rock Star signs (and expecting them) that she missed many of the subtler messages all around? Paula recently gave me the details of a heartwarming sign she did *not* miss. I think I'll end this chapter with a story she shared with me, as it's just the kind of sweet sign you may receive in your own inbox one day.

In Paula's own words:
I felt a lot of guilt about Charlie's death. We lived in separate towns, and when he took ill, I was very busy and didn't have time to drive out to see him. I had no idea he'd die so suddenly and that by waiting a week or two, I'd never see him again.

That's why I couldn't let go. The guilt was eating me alive. I was having recurring dreams in which I'd see him but could never reach him. One morning I woke up from this same dream—with Charlie totally out of reach—and wondered if there was a different way to look at this situation. Maybe there was a gift here I wasn't seeing. Maybe I needed to put on a different shade of glasses with which to view this situation.

Then I had a thought: *The next email I receive from Charlie's sister will really be from Charlie.* (It is important to note that I rarely receive emails from Charlie's sister. In fact, the only ones had been to let me know of his illness.) Fifty minutes after my declaration, I received an email from Charlie's sister! It was a chain email, the likes of which we all receive from time to time. But I absolutely *knew* this one came to me directly from Charlie. The words on my screen read:

Dear God:
The lady reading this is beautiful, classy, and strong, and I love her.
Help her live her life to the fullest.
Please promote her & cause her to excel above her expectations.
Help her shine in the darkest places where it is impossible to love.
Protect her at all times, lift her up when she needs you the most,
and let her know when she walks with you, she will always be safe.
Love you, girl!

It's always so comforting to be reminded how magical life is. The Angels we just talked about helped their loved ones move forward in times of doubt, fear, and uncertainty. I should say that it's up to each of us to do our part in receiving the love, strength, and comfort being sent to us from above.

The Sixth Fundamental: Relaxation

As you begin your journey toward connecting with the other side through welcoming and celebrating these mystical synchronicities, I want you to remember the importance of **relaxation. Relaxing your mind and body** is another **Fundamental** that's extremely important to further open the doors of communication to the spiritual world. When you're relaxed, you're more open and aware of the Subtle Signs happening all around you.

How do you relax? There are endless ways. Deep breathing, prayer, walking, listening to melodic music, meditation, yoga, hanging out in nature—or all of the above. I like to take three deep, cleansing breaths throughout the day whenever I notice that I'm getting stressed. It's fast and remarkably effective. And, when I follow them up with prayer, all the better! Make up your own relaxation techniques, or ask people you know who live a balanced life for their helpful hints.

As for communicating with your loved one, trust in your heart and just start! Perhaps the next chapter, **"Calling All Angels,"** will give you even more confidence (thus the ability to relax) in the mystical and yet completely natural practice of tapping in to this otherworldly realm.

Tips and Considerations for Receiving Signs and Messages

Lastly, in order to be open and aware of any divine messages and signs coming your way, it's good to:

- Relax your mind and body. Slow down enough that you're present to everything going on around you and within you.
- Record any Subtle Signs you receive in your Angel Journal.

- Have faith in what you see, hear, taste, smell, and feel. Stay open to the fact that those signs swirling all around you just might be sent from the one you love.
- Have fun with the signs you receive, but don't get obsessed. This is a natural process and should never be forced.
- Be grateful for the blessings you receive, and remember to say thank you.

Calling All Angels: They're Waiting; All You Have to Do Is Ask!

Is anyone out there? Before looking into this Angel business in more depth, let me ask you a general question: do you ever ask for help when you need it from your friends or family? I'm sure you do, at least occasionally. The real question is, have you ever tried asking your celestial friends who've passed on to intercede on your behalf?

If not, why not?

In this chapter we're going to look at:

1. The importance of asking for (and being open to receiving) help
2. Various Angel examples
3. Ways in which to call on your Angels (including specific prayers)

Last Survivor from 9/11

New York Port Authority worker Genelle Guzman McMillan was the last survivor pulled from the World Trade Center where nearly 3,000 people died on September 11, 2001. Only twenty people who were trapped made it out, most within several hours of the collapse.

"We could call Genelle and the others 'escapees,'" said John Cloud of *Time Magazine*, "but they didn't really escape—they just dodged fate." While still buried, Genelle began talking to God, first asking that she not suffer and then asking that her body be found so that her family could have a funeral and not be left in missing-persons limbo. Finally, her prayer was to live. She remembers a bare hand (unlike the gloved hands of the firefighters), and then a voice. "Just hold on to my hand," he said. His name? Paul. He reached through the rubble and held her hand with both of his, promising not to leave her.

Rescuers reached Genelle's dark, oven-hot tomb twenty-seven hours after the collapse and took her to a hospital, where she stayed five weeks with a bad leg injury that eventually healed despite dire medical predictions. Paul was nowhere to be seen. She asked everyone, but no one knew anything about a rescuer named Paul.

"I wasn't dreaming," she says. "I was wide awake. I know it was an Angel. That was my miracle."

———◆———

Who was Paul? I can't say for sure. But ever since learning of Genelle and her ordeal, I've wondered if her Angel, Paul, could have been Paul of Tarsus, otherwise known as Paul the Apostle or Saint Paul—the author of at least seven of the thirteen letters of the New Testament (including Romans, First Corinthians, and Hebrews). Paul, according to history, converted to Christianity on the road to Damascus, where he says in 2 Corinthians (11:32) that he himself barely escaped death.

I find it fascinating that references to Angels appear in religious texts the world over—especially in Christianity, Judaism, and Islam—where they're reported to exhibit similar, universal traits. They're often large, for instance, and enormously strong, even to the point of instilling fear in the new initiate. They can be winged, bright or shimmering, or wearing a halo. They're usually described as human in form, with a heavenly, indescribable love emanating from them. And if you've ever experienced the unconditional love of an animal, you'd swear they're also angelic (see Chapter 6 for more on this fun topic). A few other names for Angels are: Avatars from the Hindu tradition, Devas or Bodhisattvas from Buddhism, and Spirit Guides from the Native Americans.

The Greeks have a word for messenger: *angelos*. The Hebrew word for messenger, *Malakh*, also means "angel." The Persian word for angel, *angaros*, means "courier" (an official messenger) as well. One thing remains a constant: no matter the culture or faith, in times of need, Angels deliver messages and aid. It's comforting to me that these spiritual beings appear to have powers of mediation between humans and God. I don't know about you, but I like that idea.

> *You shall see the angels circling around the throne, giving glory to their Lord.*
> —*The Koran*

The New Testament talks frequently of Angels (and even Archangels—super angels, if you will). Throughout the Bible, Angels give important messages, specifically to Mary, Joseph, and the shepherds. They come to Jesus in the wilderness, visit him on the cross, are present at his tomb, and liberate the Apostles Peter and Paul (there's our Paul again) from prison.

> *For He shall give his angels charge over thee to keep thee in all thy ways.*
> —*Psalm 91:11*

Convinced yet? One could argue that the destruction of the Twin Towers was biblical in its proportions. Because Genelle was the last person to be rescued, it seems rather appropriate to me that a bonafide Angel would come to her aid.

There are books devoted to the hierarchy of Angels and all the various types of Angels, including Fallen Angels who supposedly work for the dark side (although in my humble opinion, there is no dark side—but rather places in which souls go to rest and learn and grow from past dark actions or experiences). For our purposes in this book, I'd like to cover two more specific types.

A Guardian Angel is believed to be your own personal Angel who walks with you from birth to death. The **Angel of Death,** a positive term, refers to an Angel who appears as you're preparing to leave this plane, or at the very moment of your death, escorting you to heaven, or the other side.

If you've ever spent time at the bedside of a dying person, you may have heard her talk of seeing deceased loved ones or Angels that appear to her in dreams or in person, telling her it's time. Rose was dying of pancreatic cancer and said repeatedly that her deceased mother, father, and even a stranger showed up in dreams, telling her it was time to cross over. She told each of them that she'd be ready to go with them soon but that she still had a few people to say goodbye to first. Rose lived another week, announcing to her family that she was ready on the morning of her death. I wonder if her Angels waited for Rose to complete her unfinished business simply because she asked.

This is a powerful example because it shows the importance of asking and carrying personal intention, even down to the end, a time when a person seems to have less power than ever. By stating her wish—to see certain people before she transitioned—Rose made her desire clear to the Universe.

Do You Really Ask for Help When You Need It?

I ask you to think once again about this question: **do you** really **ask for help when you need it?** If the answer is yes, do you ask for assistance with the little things in your life or only the big-ticket items? And who or what defines little versus big anyway?

My philosophy is: don't segregate the size of your needs. A need is a need. If you need help, you need help. Period.

Perhaps you carry a belief that you have to do everything on your own. I used to think that way, and it's no fun trying to be Wonder Woman. My career choice, as a computer geek and a business professional with IBM, made me all the more determined to be strong—like the boys. When I started climbing the corporate ladder as a graphics designer twenty years ago at a small engineering firm, it was a male-dominated environment. But I was okay with that. Unlike most of my girlfriends, I was a natural with numbers, facts, and sales. I soon moved up to network system administrator for the second largest financial institution in Pittsburgh, where I developed computer programs, segueing into designing, architecting, implementing, and managing a US and Canadian corporate-wide network for over thirty-five thousand users.

For the past twelve years, I've been an IBM technical sales engineer and software architect. I'm a respected and trusted coach, mentor, adviser, consultant, and professional who interfaces with people from around the world. The last thing I want is to appear weak or different. Let's just say that the fact that I happen to talk to my dead sister all day isn't really something I bring up around the conference table. But that doesn't mean I don't ask for angelic support all the time—even at the office.

So go ahead and ask. You have nothing to lose by asking, and so much to gain.

Asking Is a Sign of Strength

If you don't ask for help, how can you expect to find relief?

If you're not accustomed to asking for help, perhaps you worry that it's a sign of weakness. If so, I beg of you to please *stop* this crazy thinking, as I have. We've all lost our minds when we think we can do this life all by ourselves. Life is too fast paced, too short, and packed with too many challenges, situations, and experiences to master it on our own. We're tribal beings meant to support one another.

Try embracing this new line of thinking I've adopted: **You're being weak when you** don't **ask for help!**

I believe our Spirit Guides or Guardian Angels take great joy in lending a hand when they can (when their support serves our higher calling or purpose). For the record, I don't think they can intervene on our behalf when doing so interferes with something we're meant to go through to help us grow. I know, bummer, right? Although we may beg and plead with Spirit to give us what we think we need or want in a particular moment, we're often grateful when we have the hindsight to know we've come through those hard lessons and can see how we've grown and what we're capable of.

But it doesn't hurt to ask. Ask away. And if your gut tells you you're asking too much, try asking only when you really need relief. No one wants to get so obsessed with asking for help in every little circumstance that they can't depend on themselves in a pinch.

But sometimes there's just no other option and you desperately need *help*, like in this next story.

Saved by an Angel

It was an emotional day for Barb, typical of the previous eight months. She and her husband, Jeff, had only been married for two years, but fighting had become the norm in their household. When tempers got heated, Jeff got physical.

Barb broke the news to Jeff that she wanted a divorce, and Jeff went out with his friends. It was after midnight when she heard him return. Lying in bed, she cringed as doors began banging open and shut, until their bedroom door flew open. Through the moonlit window, she could see his glassy eyes. She held her breath and didn't move, hoping he'd turn around and close the door. Instead, Jeff started yelling.

"I know you're up. I'm not leaving," he said, calling her a few choice words. She remained frozen. Then it happened. Jeff lunged onto the bed with what she says felt like an evil force. He jumped on top of her screaming, "If I can't have you, no one can!" Jeff grabbed Barb's neck as if she were a rag doll and began choking her. She felt her life force "slipping away" and screamed inside her head for her grandmother (who had been dead several years), or God or anyone to *please help!*

Not a moment later, Barb felt a sense of power and peace wash over her. "It was immediate and mind-boggling to have this sensation of life fill me up while also being pinned down by a man who had been a professional fighter." Next, she heard her grandmother's voice: "Throw him off!" She *felt* her grandmother right by her side infusing her with remarkable strength. To Barb's surprise, she threw Jeff off of her as if tossing a ball into the air. Jeff went flying across the room and landed on the floor, up against the dresser, dazed and confused.

Barb flew out of bed and ran down the hallway toward the front door. Shaking and unable to think clearly, she stood in the living room in shock, scared for her life. She looked up. He was walking down the hall toward her, a smirk across his face. "Stay away from me," Barb screamed. "I'm calling the police." She hoped that would stop him, but she didn't even have the phone in her hand. *Oh God, please help me get out of here. Please save me!*

Jeff was fast approaching. As he entered the living room, Barb braced herself for a physical fight. But miraculously, out of the blue, he turned around, opened the door leading to the game room, and walked downstairs.

Oh my God, really?! Thank you so much, she prayed. Moving fast now, she grabbed her cell phone and keys. Her hands were shaking so hard that it seemed an eternity before she could unlatch the door. *Gram, please, please help me get out of here safely!* As she swung the door open, Barb was relieved when a stroke of incredible "luck" found her car parked in front of the house versus in the garage. Normally Jeff's truck would be blocking hers in the driveway, but earlier she had forgotten to pull her car in. As Barb sped off in her car, she called her best friend, hysterical, saying she was on her way. Once at her friend's house, they quickly hid Barb's car in the garage. Shortly afterward, Barb's cell phone began ringing off the hook; Jeff called too many times to count. When she finally answered, it was to tell him the police were on their way.

"I know where you are. I know your car is in her garage. You think I'm stupid? I'm going to ram my truck into her house and kill all of you." The police arrived—six black-and-whites filled the driveway and the street. Barb felt safe for the moment, but she knew that once the police left, Jeff could do anything. She called Jeff's best friend, Bill, and explained what had happened and begged him to find Jeff and take him home. Luckily, Bill had a way to reel Jeff in, and he took Jeff to his house for the night to calm down.

Barb knew that her grandmother and God had come to her aid that night, and she accessed this same feeling of angelic safety to find the courage to file for divorce. Barb and Jeff still argued a few times after the incident, but he never turned violent again. They went their separate ways, and because they didn't have children, that was the last of it. Barb is now happily remarried and living in another state.

Where did Barb get the power to throw off her raging husband, despite his choke hold around her throat? **Why did he suddenly go downstairs** for a few minutes versus going after Barb in his rage? **Why did she park her car on the road** instead of in the garage as usual?

Barb swears it was because she has always prayed and felt a deep spiritual connection with God and her grandmother. She asked for help that night and was consequently protected, but she had also been guided to perform certain actions, like parking on the street, which prepared her to escape something she didn't even know was coming.

Something to Consider

You could get a stomachache reading Barb's story about the violence she endured. Perhaps you've experienced something similar that drastically affected your life. But I want you to consider that Barb's experience changed her life for the *better*. In fact, she says she wouldn't even think to erase it from her history, as it revealed a strength she never knew she had. One of the gifts of Barb's marriage was that during the challenging times, she spent many days and nights praying for guidance, talking to her grandmother, and hoping for assistance. She couldn't have seen past the negativity without asking for and being open to receiving help from her grandmother and the Divine. Experiencing their support changed her life forever. This is the power and the beauty of spiritual connections with the other side. And it's all simply a thought away.

There are other less dramatic, but still emotional, reasons to call on your Angel friends. There may be times you'll want to call on angelic support for matters of the heart, as my client Jennifer once did.

Calling All License Plates

Jennifer was finally falling in love after years of being alone. Her husband of twenty-five years had had an affair, and it had taken Jen a long time to love again. She'd met Dan online, and they'd hit it off. It had only been a few months, but they both knew this was soul-mate love—the relationship they'd each waited a lifetime for.

But Jennifer had a big problem. Dan had a weekend wife. Well, not really a wife, but a girlfriend he saw on weekends that he just couldn't shake. He'd been meaning to break up with her and had long since stopped being intimate with her—even before Jennifer came into the picture. But the girlfriend had been going through a tough time at work, and with her being a single mother Dan didn't have the heart to tell her he wanted out. He was stalling, thinking that if he waited a bit longer, he could find a "good" time to let her down. He saw her briefly on weekends, coached her son in Little League, and then raced home as quickly as he could to see Jen.

Jennifer was a mess. She refused to see Dan, not wanting to be the other woman. Her friends begged her to date other men, calling Dan a player. Jen knew in her heart that Dan was a good man, and she believed his intentions were honorable toward her, the girlfriend, *and* the child, but she was lonely and starting to question if she could hold on. The stress often left her crying herself to sleep.

One night Jen went for a walk. She missed Dan so much and wondered what to do. She decided to ask for help. Her parents had each been dead over a decade, and now was as good a time as any to ask for their guidance.

"Mom, Dad," she prayed aloud, "please tell me—from your vantage point, is Dan even worth it? Is he a good guy? Do you even like him?"

Jennifer heard her own voice in her head say, *Check the license plate on the white car coming up ahead, and you will have our answer.* It was dark out, but she could see a white car parked up ahead, about a block away. She walked up to the car and read the plate: 4DSJ22L. She gasped. Dan's initials were D. S. She felt within her heart a strong sense, or knowing, that the 4 stood for "We are for him." Immediately she felt she had her answer. Her parents were indeed "for" the man she loved, and she would wait for him.

For the first time in weeks, Jen felt renewed hope and breathed a sigh of relief. Ten days after asking her parents for advice, Dan broke up with his girlfriend and fully committed to Jennifer, taking her to Hawaii a month later to thank her for being so patient. It's been nearly two years, and they're engaged and very much in love.

Jennifer told me that the hardest part of that time for her was that everyone was telling her something she knew in her heart wasn't true—that he was playing her. "I wanted to follow my heart," she says, "but had I not asked for guidance and received such a clear sign, I may not have trusted my heart. I could have become angry and easily blown it with this man. Relationship experts were telling me to turn away, and that was hard to tune out."

Life just works better when we follow the guidance from within, from our heart. Jennifer's happy life with this man who adores her and takes care of her in a way no man ever has is a testament to that trust. As I tell my clients, your heart knows only truth; your mind and ego typically remain in a place of fear and mistrust. It's up to you to tune in to your heart and allow it to lead you. Your internal wisdom—strengthened, I believe, by benevolent spiritual guidance from beyond—will always steer you to your highest purpose.

The Power of Prayer

Prayer is the most powerful tool each of us has at our disposal any time of the day or night. There is no right or wrong way to pray. It can be quiet or aloud, written, sung, or in your head—whatever feels comfortable to you. It's easy. Asking for help from your deceased loved one or God, or a higher power, won't take you but a minute or two. It's free, and it doesn't require any skill other than asking, watching, and listening.

I love praying to my sister and God all the time. If I'm standing in the grocery aisle and don't know what vitamin to buy, I'll ask for a hint quietly under my breath. Then I watch and listen. If a bottle appears to jump out at me or seems a little brighter somehow, I pay attention. If I have a hunch or an intuition to do something, go somewhere, or slow down, I listen to that, too.

Nonbelievers could argue that I'm being crazy, talking to a spiritual form whose existence can't necessarily be proven. Just for argument's sake, let's pretend they're right. Why would it matter? These prayers feel therapeutic. They energize me. They remind me to take notice of the many blessings in my life. They make me feel supported and less alone. If the good mood they instill isn't real, then I'd prefer to be the last to know. My spirits are lifted, life works, and I'm happy. I choose to believe prayer changes everything.

I believe it's okay to ask for help with anything—even with getting you through your to-do list with ease, with having enough patience to deal with your children, or with providing you more energy and confidence to accomplish a goal. Even help with finding a lost item.

Seek and Ye Shall Find

Shortly after my sister's death, while I was still in high school, I wore her school ring along with mine. I usually caught a ride to school with my best friend's mom, and during the drive, I'd often take my rings off and use the hand lotion she stored in the glove compartment. I'd set my rings on my lap and then put them back on after applying the lotion. One day I forgot to put them back on; they fell from my lap, but I later found them on the floor of the car. A few weeks later, I did the same thing. This time, the rings weren't in the car. I prayed to my sister to bring them back to me, and the next morning, I found them on the street outside of our school. This was a very busy thorough-fare traveled by hundreds of kids. What were the odds that they'd still be there? That's my kind of divine intervention.

Through the rich, deep, and profoundly healing connection I have with Kathy, I am certain that the veil between here and there is gossamer, and that anyone—regardless of belief or station—can receive guidance and grow closer to a loved one who has crossed over, perhaps to an even greater extent than in life. For me, ever since my sister's death in 1987, not only have I grown closer to her, I've also come to see that every decision, risk, adventure, accomplishment, deed, job, presentation, award, relationship, and experience—basically everything in my life—has been impacted and inspired by my relationship with my sister and her heavenly guidance.

These spiritual connections, available to anyone, are so loving, comforting, powerful, and special on so many levels that they influence every area of my life—not just in dealing with the other side. They make everything more meaningful.

One way I really feel connected with my sister is by stepping out in nature when no one else is around. I allow my body to relax and get very still, where the swaying of the trees in the gentle breeze reminds me that heaven is all around. *All is right in my life. All is calm.*

If I'm inside, I'll play soft music or meditation recordings as I light a candle, maybe take a bath. It's all about giving myself the time to relax and breathe deeply. Each time I do this, I allow myself to be a little more open to spirituality, to the Divine, to a higher power, and to my loved ones on the other side. Each time I do this, I remember how delicious life is, and how we always get exactly what we need.

Life Is Magical

A young woman, Missy, now in her thirties, grew up close to her Uncle Wayne. In high school, she'd moved in with him and his wife when her mother had to leave the school district and Missy wanted to finish up where she'd started. Missy and her uncle were more than just family; they were friends. She confided in him as if he were her own father. When her uncle took ill, Missy didn't have the courage to face him. She feared death, and she didn't want to remember him as a sickly person. When her uncle did lose his life, Missy felt intense guilt about not visiting him during his illness, and she worried that he died not knowing how much she loved him.

Several months after his passing, Missy was depressed and incredibly stressed about her financial situation. Taxes were due, and she couldn't pay them. She fell asleep praying to God, her uncle, and to heaven to please help. She dreamed of her Uncle Wayne; he walked up to her at a party and gave her two $5,100 bills. She remembers laughing in the dream, saying, "There's no such thing as a $5,100 bill, Uncle Wayne!" He looked her square in the face and said, "Just trust me." At that moment, she woke up.

Sitting up in amazement, she wondered what the dream could have meant, and she turned to look at her husband. She couldn't believe her eyes; her uncle's face was pressed against her husband's sleeping face, cheek-to-cheek. It was the perfect picture of her uncle; he looked so happy and healthy and mischievous. She so badly wanted to shake her husband and tell him what she'd seen on his face, but she was too mesmerized to move.

Her uncle's image lasted only for a brief moment, but the sensation of warmth and peace stayed with her. When her husband awoke, she told him of the dream, and they decided to play the lottery. Three days in a row, Missy and her husband played the number 5100. On the third day, they won $10,000!

"I couldn't believe it," Missy said. "Obviously he held no ill will that I hadn't seen him while he was sick. It's as if he was right here all along, protecting me in death as he had in life."

The Seventh Fundamental: Beliefs

In wrapping up this chapter, let's talk about a key **Fundamental: Beliefs.** Every synchronicity, every seeming coincidence, every premonition, every knowing is real. If you're having a bit of a challenge receiving communication from your loved ones on the other side, perhaps it will help you to take a moment to evaluate what beliefs you're living by. We discussed this in the chapter on Faith, but deep-rooted beliefs of how something should (or should not) work out could still be blocking your connections from blossoming. Even those on this side.

When I see or assume this is happening with a client, one of the first questions I ask is, "Do you *really* believe it's possible to connect with the other side?" No matter how faithful we are, we all have some beliefs we adopted as kids and others we've chosen as adults. Some clash. In order to open the doors to heavenly communication, seeing where you're thwarting your own effort is very helpful. If, for example, your parents didn't believe in an afterlife, even if you do, you may have trouble talking to the other side—and perhaps you don't even realize why you feel a bit embarrassed, unworthy, or fraudulent. The best you can do is move forward with an open mind and release any fears, judgments, or disbeliefs you harbor. Maybe say a prayer to release limiting beliefs you're not even conscious of so that you can let go and stay open to all the positive possibilities.

Remember, too, that your loved ones are no longer bound by the laws of physics and are therefore accessible anytime, anywhere to provide you the boost of whatever you may need. Think of them as members of your own heavenly cheering section—ready and willing to help out when they can, and when they're not interfering with a greater plan.

Tips and Considerations for Reaching Out to the Other Side:

- Believe! Believe in yourself and your ability to receive messages and signs from the other side; believe in a power greater than you to help you along life's path.
- Ask, ask, ask. If you don't ask, how can you ever expect to receive?
- Know that you deserve greatness, because you do. Everyone does!
- God needs His Angels—including your loved one—by His side. Isn't it heartening to know that you have a loved one with God who knows and understands firsthand your challenges here on earth—allowing her to better support you?
- When you have nowhere else to turn, your loved one is only a thought away.
- It's time to experience what's already all around you—heaven on earth!

❦ 6 ❧

From Bugs to Bugs Bunny: Connecting with Critters and Creatures

Ever wonder if your cat or bunny or bird has a soul? If you're a proud dog or horse owner, you might swear that when they stare at you with their big, beautiful eyes, they're indeed more soulful than most people you know.

As you might guess, I have plenty of thoughts on the soulful nature of animals. I have no doubt that animals are no less important to God and the Angels than humans are, and that they not only have a soul that lives on but that, dead or alive, they're busy communicating with us and sending us messages all the time—and they even protect us from harm. The magic and power of animals is worth being open to, especially when reaching out to the spiritual world.

In this chapter, I share stories that just might make you look at animals—insects, even—in a different light. Rather than focusing merely on their death, we'll also look at how they can help us in our life to be open to otherworldly guidance, and even how our loved ones may use their form to touch our hearts. I firmly believe that God's critters are working hand-in-hand with our loved ones to deliver important messages to us. Sometimes we need something out of the ordinary to catch our attention and snap us out of our trance. Animals can do this.

There are many well-documented stories of animals protecting humans. A pod of dolphins saves a surfer's life from a ravenous great white shark. A gorilla protects a five-year-old boy who falls into a concrete gorilla enclosure at the zoo. A dog lies across a four-year-old girl throughout the night, protecting her and keeping her warm until the search party can rescue her the next day. How do they know we're in trouble? Why do they care? And do they continue loving and protecting us even after they're gone? Maybe, like Angels, they're all part of God's bigger plan.

To kick things off, let's look at an example of an animal Rock Star moment. Yes, even our four-legged friends appear to have a flair for the dramatic.

Leo Rocks the House

Gina, her big sister, and their parents were obsessed with their only dog—a beautiful, vibrant German shepherd named Leo. At eight years old, Leo contracted kidney disease. It was a quick and devastating decline that culminated at the veterinarian's office, where the family bawled and gathered around Leo as he had a seizure and had to be put down.

Gina was a teenager and had never had an animal before, so Leo's tragic passing was brutal for her. But it was even harder on her mother. Although they were a spiritual family and knew that it must be his time, and they even believed they'd see Leo again one day, their hearts and intellects were miles apart. Nothing seemed to relieve their grief. Even a year later, Gina's mother would still cry every time she saw another big dog while driving or walking through their neighborhood. "I can never get another animal," she'd say. "I couldn't stand to go through that kind of pain ever again." Needless to say, Gina and her mother weren't letting him go. They had lost much of the joy in their family life, and they didn't seem to know how to get beyond their grief.

When Leo was alive, he was a large, eighty-five-pound dog with an unusual habit. When he wanted inside from the backyard, he'd thrust his heavy frame against the sliding glass door in their dining room. He'd stand on his hind legs and rock the glass back and forth with his front paws while the family was eating brunch or dinner. It was a loud, bad habit, but they loved his energy and enthusiasm (they considered him to be saying hello), and thought it was darling—marveling at their good fortune that the safety glass never came crashing down.

After a particularly hard week for Gina and her mother, where they'd been crying about how much they still missed him, Gina was at the house by herself. She stood at the dining room table and was going through the mail when the sliding glass door suddenly began to rock wildly back and forth. They lived in earthquake country in the Bay Area of Northern California—only seventy minutes from San Francisco—so Gina assumed they were having an earthquake and ran outside. But once she got in the front yard and looked around, nothing else was moving. She slowly walked back into the house and saw that the glass was still rocking back and forth. Something whispered to Gina that it was Leo; that he was trying to get her attention.

Gina said she immediately knew what Leo wanted. He wanted Gina and her mother to know that he had moved on and that they, too, needed to move forward with their lives and stop grieving. They were holding him back through their grief, and he needed to be released. When her mother came home from work, Gina told her what had happened, and they decided to stay strong together. This mother and daughter never mourned another day. Their love for their dog and his needs was all it took to jolt them out of their suffering. It was a choice for Gina and her mother to let go of the heavy energy that was weighing everybody down. Doing so seemed to set them all on a better path. They stopped crying and felt only joy when they thought of Leo, and the sliding glass door stayed forever silent.

Losing a pet can be utterly devastating, sometimes harder than having to say goodbye to a human. Human relationships are often complicated—encompassing the vast range of emotions, both positive and negative. Our relationships with our animals, however, often feel more pure-hearted and sacred. Pets are so unconditionally loving that, for some of us, they're the most kind and gentle relationships we'll ever have. Their innocence opens our hearts, and their deaths can crush our world. There's the fact, too, that in many cases, our dying human loved ones may have the time and ability to say goodbye. But that's not the case with our pets. We put them down or watch them die, never truly knowing if they're emotionally ready, what they're thinking, or if we're acting in accordance with their wishes. It can be agonizing.

As you saw with Gina and Leo, desperation can freeze both parties in place. With their new understanding, Gina and her mother didn't forget about Leo—they still talk about him and even to him. But their grief made way for a celebration of his life and memory. In their *choice* to let Leo's spirit fly, he is now free to love and guide them in new ways. Bravo to him—his Rock Star antics couldn't have been clearer.

You will go through your own experiences with animals, whether you connect with them after they've passed, as Gina did, or while they're still here and very much alive. Let's take a look at the subtle ways in which animals or insects may touch our hearts or bring important messages to us.

The Prayerful Praying Mantis

I was sitting at a baseball game with some friends, two rows behind the opposing team's dugout. It was a typical game—loud with fans clapping, cheering, and yelling. Out of nowhere, a praying mantis jumped up on my friend's leg. My initial reaction was to scream at the top of my lungs and smack it away because I've never been one for insects, especially large ones.

But in the second before I could act on my instincts, I felt goose bumps cover my arms and legs, and I experienced one of those invisible hugs I sometimes feel from above. I had a powerful sense that this little guy was a blessing, that he was here to give a sign of some sort to my friend and me.

The praying mantis stayed put for a few minutes and then jumped onto my leg. Boy, did that ever freak me out! But I went with it because, through all of the commotion of the fans clapping and cheering and standing up and sitting down all around us, this praying mantis didn't move.

A few minutes later, the praying mantis jumped back onto my friend's leg.

"This must mean something big," my friend said. I agreed, but we had no idea what. He then jumped onto the roof of the dugout, closest to the row of seats in front of us, facing the field. Within seconds, however, the praying mantis turned around and stared at us.

I kid you not when I say that he literally sat there for the remainder of the game—all thirty minutes of it—looking straight at us without moving. It felt as if he was reading our souls, or transmitting something spiritual to us.

I picked up my cell phone and called a friend to look up the meaning of *praying mantis medicine* online because we had to know what this meant. (By *medicine* I mean a Native American term that refers to spiritual gifts given to us for our betterment.) I hadn't even seen one of these insects for thirty years and had certainly never seen an insect act like this in a crowded place. She told me that *mantis* is the Greek word for "prophet" or "seer," and the insect has long been thought by native peoples to be a spiritual being with mystical powers. It sure seemed like it to us, as he sat there with his front legs in the prayer position.

"He represents the need to be still, settle down, and meditate," my friend continued to read. "Be mindful of different decisions and actions in your life," she said. I thought about what this might mean for me. My first son had just been born, and during the year before his birth, I had been receiving signs that my life's purpose would be changing, that I was no longer supposed to work so hard in my career. I felt as if this was yet another way the Universe was letting me know that I was headed down a spiritual path of helping others.

I can look back now and clearly see the spiritual aftereffects of this visit. I'm living my spiritual journey now, and this book is one of the outcomes of this shift in my life.

You may have your own story of how an animal or insect has brought you comfort, lifted your spirits, guided you to what's next, or even saved you. However, it's not always easy to place the meaning of messages or signs from animals or insects when they occur, but your heart will tell you if there's something you need to pay attention to, as mine did that day at the game. Even though I couldn't pinpoint the exact details, I still felt strongly that the praying mantis was speaking to us and delivering some type of message that would one day be clear. I found this clarity months later, and I continue to see its message even today.

Once again, my advice is to stay open to the gifts and guidance all around you. I think it's important to be open to benevolent guidance wherever it comes from and to be aware of the power that comes from animals both dead and alive. Now, let's cover animal totems—something native peoples worldwide know intimately.

Animal Totems

The concept of animals as spiritual guides, teachers, or protectors has a long history. Power animals, or totems, are a shamanic concept whereby Spirit Guides help and protect people. In this native worldview, everything—including rocks and trees—is alive and has wisdom to share. In connecting with one's power animal(s), a person can then benefit from the qualities inherent to that animal as well as access their power.

As spiritual beings, animals are highly attuned to Spirit, unlike us humans, who are more easily influenced by the world and therefore more disconnected from our spiritual selves. Animals' ability to sense their owners' emotions and provide comfort, and to sense danger and protect us, is absolutely remarkable. (Next time you are having a bad day, pay attention to how your dog or cat responds to you. I've had many days where I was hurting inside, but no one noticed on the surface because I put on my happy face. That never fooled my dog. She would stay by my side and place her paw on my leg and look at me lovingly.) I truly believe our animals are connected to the Divine at very deep levels and see into dimensions that most humans haven't learned to see (or have unlearned). It's telling that *dog* is *God* spelled backwards, don't you think?

Each totem animal represents significant energy and provides different kinds of support. A wealth of books have been written describing the goal of each totem, and you can also look up the meaning of individual animals online by Googling "the meaning of . . ." My point is, critters come in and out of your life (just as humans do) to deliver messages to you, influence you, provide you guidance, or lend a paw for what's coming next. If you recognize an animal appearing and reappearing in your life, or an insect that keeps circling your body, for instance, chances are there's a message in it for you. And this message could very well be from your loved one delivered to you via the critter. I encourage you to research what you're experiencing for further information, but the following are a few of my favorite totems.

Hummingbirds are known to appear in greater abundance when people are outside praying to a deceased loved one. If you think about what hummingbirds do in nature, they literally suck nectar from flowers so that more of its kind can be born. Talk about a beautiful job, and a happy one! In fact, many Native Americans think hummingbirds represent joy. So, the next time you're crying to a loved one who has passed away and a hummingbird flies overhead, see if you can't turn that frown upside down.

Butterflies are all about transformation. As the *only* living beings that change their entire genetic structure in the maturation process from one form to another (caterpillar to butterfly), they're the symbol of transformation and life after death, and they're a treasured sign for people wanting assurance that their deceased loved ones are okay or that they themselves are being watched over. When you next see a butterfly, think about what message it might be bringing you about your own protection or transformation.

Ladybugs are a symbol of good luck. What child or adult doesn't love seeing their bright little bodies fly through the air and land on them? Ladybugs, with their tiny wings and black spots, can eat thousands of aphids in their short four-month life span, and they have long been a favored omen for farmers in protecting their crops. Next time you see one, make a wish and have fun thinking about your good fortune and the good fortune you and your loved one shared together.

Hawks are my favorite totem. These visionaries and messengers are said to deliver messages from the Great Spirit (or Holy Spirit) and are akin to Angels. With their ability to soar high above the land, they can touch both Spirit and the earth at the same time. These big-picture birds remind us to set our sights high and not allow ourselves to get tied down by our limitations and earthly burdens.

The above examples are but a few. Again, when going about your life, if you notice an animal trying to get your attention, perk up and watch or listen because there could be a message in it for you. (A friend of mine once saw an ant climb up on her sink faucet, stand on its hind legs, and wave its front legs toward her wildly. She thought about what the ant symbolized—work, work, work—and remembered that she had forgotten to take care of important business for a client earlier in the day, something that could have hurt her and her client if it weren't handled.) Open your eyes, heart, and mind to connecting with your four-legged, winged, and feathered friends. It can be extremely rewarding.

Maybe, just maybe, they want to bring you a comforting message, a validation, or a sign of confirmation from the other side.

Signs Come Flying In

My friend Melony believed she'd found her soul mate. Every minute they spent together felt so right and blissful that she questioned if their connection could possibly be real—or if she was fabricating important details of their union.

Melony is on a spiritual path and has no problem asking for signs as confirmation or for clarification. This time was no different. She asked for validation for this powerful love that had entered her life. She wanted to make sure what she felt was from her heart and not her ego.

Always drawn to animals, Melony believed she could receive messages from them. She sat down in her living room one morning, took a big deep breath, and said to herself, "What animal should be my sign to tell me if this love is indeed real?" At the moment she completed her prayer, a red cardinal landed on the tree right outside her window. Melony had never seen a red cardinal near her house. As it sat perched on a branch facing her window, she felt as if it was staring through her soul. Melony knew that the red cardinal was the critter who came to work with her.

She then made an intention. "If I see a red cardinal over the next day, this will be confirmation that what I feel within my heart is indeed truth. If I don't see a red cardinal in the next day, I will know my ego (mind) has made me feel as if this illusionary love is real."

I know it may seem silly to do something like this, but because animals, birds, and insects are all around and are so connected, asking for signs is a simple exercise. Why not engage them so the transfer of messages and the communication is easier to understand? And, if you don't get a sign, perhaps you weren't meant to know the answer at that time. Or you need to figure it out on your own, following your own guidance.

Melony continued forward with her day as usual. She went to work, drove home at the end of the day, ate dinner, and then decided to head outdoors to weed in her yard. While gathering up the weed killer, garbage bags and gloves, she looked down the driveway into her yard just as two red cardinals came flying toward her. One right after the other, they looked as if they were playing and chasing each other. They flew so close to Melony's shoulder that she actually felt the wind from their wings on her face. A chill ran up and down her spine. "It was as if they passed some of their love on to me as they flew by," she said.

Not only did Melony see a red cardinal. She saw *two* red cardinals—playing, flying, and whistling through the air. She shook her head and laughed. She already knew the love she felt was real, but this beautiful sign with the two red cardinals was certainly a great gift of validation.

I love how the Universe and Spirit add that extra little touch to get their point across so we can ditch our doubt!

Butterfly to the Rescue

When my oldest son was a little over two and a half years old, we took a vacation to a lake. Several of us were planning to water-ski, and others would inner tube behind the boat. My son declared that he wanted to give tubing a try. I was determined to encourage his youthful confidence, even though I wanted to pass out at the thought of something going wrong. Visions of the tube flipping over and traumatizing him for all future water sports ran in a continuous loop in my mind. But I sucked it up and carried on.

The first time I got in the water and sat down on the tube, I went to reach for my son and flipped the tube over myself. Well, that's what I get for thinking about flipping over! At least it happened to me, and *only* me.

My panic had now increased, and I needed to settle myself down. I started praying to my sister and to God to please just let everything work out great, and allow us to have a fun, safe time. I imagined us staying securely in the tube throughout the entire ride.

When I was finally able to secure my son in the tube with me, I was just about ready to (reluctantly) signal for the boat to move when I looked up to see the most beautiful butterfly I'd ever seen, floating only about six inches above our heads. I got goose bumps all over. *Where did this butterfly come from? We are literally in the middle of a mile-and-a-half wide lake!* That might not seem wild to you, but to me, it was awesome confirmation that we would be protected.

The butterfly flew with us for about a minute until the boat picked up speed, seeming to stick around until I felt comfortable that my young son and I would be safe. I can't tell you how comforting its presence was, literally enabling me to relax and laugh and get out of my head enough to drop down into my body and thoroughly enjoy the ride. I was even able to notice the little things—the way the sun sparkled off the surface of the water, how the people in the boat were cheering us on, and how radiant my son looked as he clutched my arm with his tiny hands and squealed for his uncle to go faster.

While it seems improbable that God or the Angels or even my sister could have sent that butterfly to comfort me, I think of how Genelle (from Chapter 5) was comforted by that stranger for the long hours she was trapped in the rubble of the Twin Towers. It makes me think that if an actual Angel in human form could materialize to hold a woman's hands during her life-and-death crisis, why couldn't a small butterfly come to comfort a worried mother?

I like to think we're all connected and worthy of love, comfort, and assurances from the Divine.

Now with that said, our animals and insect friends aren't always warm and fuzzy with their support. Sometimes their form of guidance, although helpful, is anything but comforting.

The Bumblebee Dive-Bomber

Paula, a woman in her fifties, had lost the love of her life three years prior. One evening, she was enjoying dinner on her patio with a man who had also lost his significant other. During conversations about their lives and losses, Paula began speaking ill of her brother-in-law, who had also recently passed.

"He was such a mean, nasty person," she said, revealing details to justify her feelings. Suddenly, out of nowhere, a hornet wasp began dive-bombing their table and wouldn't leave, no matter what they tried. They moved around and still, the hornet followed. Finally, they had to use bug spray to get rid of it. Paula realized that she'd been talking negatively about her brother-in-law and stopped, changing the subject to loving comments about other departed loved ones.

A moment after this shift in conversation, a beautiful butterfly came and hovered around them for about twenty minutes, flitting over their table. It would fly away and then come right back. Paula had a strong feeling her loved ones could hear their conversation and were confirming their love back to her. Needless to say, she was grateful the night ended with the lovely, peaceful butterfly after the scary hornet attack.

If you're wondering why a hornet would dive-bomb someone, a quick online search reveals that hornet medicine stops negative situations. I like to imagine that the brother-in-law was saying that he knows he wasn't perfect while here on earth but he wants to rest in peace. I imagine that he wants everyone to move on and accept what was, as well as the fact that he is now a spiritual being living in love. It seems likely, too, that the butterfly came to help Paula change the energy toward her brother-in-law and to validate the goodness in the way she was now talking about those she missed.

The moral of this story? Stop for a moment before assuming something bad is happening to you, or that someone (dead or alive) is out to get you. Make a habit of looking for the goodness in all your experiences. We're too quick to zero in on what appears to be negative. Remember, every experience helps us grow as individuals. It's up to us to look beyond the surface to recognize the messages and signs coming in. Paula helped herself feel better and grow from the dive bombing hornet because she realized it wasn't something bad happening *to* her; it was instead a message for her to stop judging and talking negatively about others so she could then focus on the beauty in her life.

The Beloved Dog Who Never Dies

The most miraculous animal story of life after death I've ever heard comes from a very close business colleague of mine. She's well-known in her field and for that, I will change her name and the names of her family members because the story is so "out there" that she's asked me to protect her anonymity. I'll call her Tammy.

Tammy had a border collie named Sandy. Border collies are working sheep-herding breeds, bred to run many miles a day. A lifelong athlete herself, Tammy loved to walk or run at least five miles a day, so from the time Sandy was a pup, that's what they did. Tammy, her husband, and their son took Sandy in the car with them nearly everywhere they went. Everyone adored this dog and delighted in seeing her whenever they could.

"She didn't even need a leash," Tammy said. "It's like she was human. If we asked her to go sit in the corner, she'd do it. If we asked her to go into the other room, off she'd go. She loved all other dogs, cats, people—you name it. It was uncanny how devoted and lovable and human-like she was."

Their friends used to say that whenever Sandy eventually died, Tammy wouldn't be able to handle it—especially because her husband had said, "No more dogs." Replacing her would be a "deal breaker" for their marriage, he said. He wanted to live five years "at least" without having to care for another animal. So, three years before Sandy showed any sign of illness, Tammy actually had a few therapy sessions to deal with her fear of the inevitable loss. She'd already lost her folks to cancer, and she knew how to deal with the pain of intense heartbreak. But this was different. Sandy was her daily companion, her shadow. There wouldn't be a replacement coming to fill the void, and it was clear to all that this was going to be one of, if not *the*, biggest challenge of Tammy's life.

When the time was close, Tammy's friend, an animal psychic, said: "Don't worry. Sandy is tired, but she's going to come back to you in another dog."

"That's impossible," Tammy said. "John will never allow it."

"Oh, John is not a problem. Sandy will come to him. He will know her from her eyes, and he won't be able to resist her. You will have her again within about a year, and he will think it was his idea."

When Sandy died of old age at sixteen, Tammy was as ready as she could be. She was heartbroken, as were her husband and son, but she knew Sandy had lived a great life, and she accepted that it was her time. She believed Sandy would find a way back to their home, even though she questioned how she would ever be able to weasel into John's now closed-to-dogs heart.

Nearly a year later, the dog psychic visited.

"Tammy, I just saw the most beautiful dog in the world walking around the corner to your house. Seriously, she's unbelievable. You need to see her." Out of curiosity, Tammy looked outside and saw a little fluff of a toy poodle walking with someone she'd never seen before. Poodles were not her style, nor were little dogs. But she had to admit; this was the cutest face she'd ever seen. Oddly, she had the markings of a border collie, with a white stripe down her face (something her veterinarian would later say he'd never seen before in a purebred poodle). Turns out, the eighty-two-year-old woman who lived down the street had purchased the dog for her ailing husband to cheer him up. Their live-in nurse was walking the dog around the block for her first official outing after having been cooped up in a cage for nearly a year.

Tammy ran out to meet the dog, but then she didn't see her again for several months. One day her husband ran into the house. "I just saw Sandy! I swear, this little poodle is her! I can see it in her eyes. And she's got all of Sandy's mannerisms."

The gist of what happened is that the old woman was spending so much time at the hospital that she regretted ever getting the dog in the first place. She was asking all the neighbors if they wanted to take her. Nearly everyone wanted the little fluff ball named Marina, so John started a two-month campaign to convince the woman to choose their family.

The old woman did end up choosing them. Marina's new family would walk her down to visit the old woman nightly for many years. In short, it was love, love, love all around. But here's the *real* magic of the story: One day, not long after getting Marina, Tammy was on the phone with her psychic friend, saying, "Marina's so much like Sandy, even down to the unique way in which Sandy chewed her food and played with tennis balls, but could it really, really be Sandy come back to life? That's so hard to imagine."

Just then, Tammy's ten-year-old son came walking in the room. He had been collecting all sorts of game cards for years and handed her a Pokémon card, saying, "Mom. Look at this. Could this be a sign?"

The card was a drawing of a brown toy poodle that looked *exactly* like Marina, complete with an M on its gold dog-bone nameplate on its collar (the same M nametag Marina came with). Tammy couldn't believe her eyes, but she screamed when she read the writing on the Pokéman card for the dog named Marron (unbelievably close to Marina). The card said: "When this card is sent to your graveyard, it is returned to your deck."

Dad in a Dog Suit

You just never know how connected animals are to you or how they will touch your heart in the future. If you're not a believer yet, maybe this story will open your mind (or make you laugh).

My husband's father passed away, and two weeks after he was gone, my husband answered a knock at our door. My own father and my sister Cindy had come to our house to babysit.

But there was another visitor with them, a dog. A very unique-looking dog, in that he had black fur with a mix of brown fur throughout—sort of like cat fur. At any rate, this was a dog none of us had ever seen before, nor since. He was beautiful, and he jumped all around with excitement.

My father and sister explained that as soon as they pulled into our driveway, the dog immediately ran up to my sister. They were initially frightened because they weren't sure if the dog was friendly. "But after the shock of the dog running up to me," Cindy said, "I had an immediate peaceful feeling. I knew the dog was safe and that he was here for a purpose."

My husband tried opening the door for my sister and dad, but every time he did, the dog tried to come into the house. My husband, being a dog owner most of his life, used the command, "No!" Typically when domesticated dogs hear this command, they stop in their tracks. But not this dog. Instead, he happily jumped up and down, pushing on the door to get into our home. He wasn't aggressive at all, though. He was very gentle, entirely cheerful, while doing everything he could to get inside. When my husband closed the door, the dog would pat the door and look into the long glass window with a big smile on his face. It was wild. He would then run out into the front yard, right up to my sister, and then back to the door.

Once my dad and sister were inside, the dog patted the door once or twice more, and then he ran off. He disappeared, and we've never seen him since. Later that evening, my husband looked at me and said, "You know, that was my dad coming to let me know he's okay. I just know it. I could feel it. It was weird, but a good feeling."

My heart smiled so big because, prior to our relationship, my husband didn't believe much in life after death. He has since become a believer because of the many situations he's been blessed to experience.

This dog touched my husband's heart for what he needed that night, and also my sister's heart for what she needed—a friendly burst of love! Animals provide so much to us. All we have to do is remember to keep our eyes, ears, and hearts open for their gentle, loving, mystical messages.

Messages in the Sky

Before closing the chapter, I leave you with a story that shows the power of animal medicine when you've lost hope. We often feel this way when we lose someone near and dear.

In Dr. Bill's own words:

For several years now, I've been following guidance and signs from God or Spirit that have helped me greatly on my spiritual journey and evolution. A number of the signs I've received have come through animals. Being part Cherokee Indian, I'm quite familiar with animal medicine. Therefore, I pay close attention to the animals' actions that seem out of the norm because usually it's signifying that there's a message being communicated.

On one particular summer day in July 2010, I received several powerful messages from our feathered friends, the hawks, which literally turned my life around.

At the time I received these messages, I was going through a very low point in my life. I had virtually lost everything, was homeless and living in a tent on a friend's property. My business had failed, and due to the economy, I was unable to raise the capital I needed to continue with the business. I was going through an ugly divorce and couldn't find work anywhere in the country, although I had interviewed with companies from coast to coast. There wasn't much need for a PhD chemist, and I was simply overqualified. Despite all of this heartache, I was surviving and managing to keep things going through odd jobs and being a handyman on the property.

During this dark time, I began exploring my Native American heritage by attending sweat lodges and asking for signs and visions to guide me on my journey. I received many, one of which was around identifying my true Indian name. In Native American tradition, there are two ways to receive your Indian name. One is to go through a formal naming ceremony; the other is to come by your name through signs and visions. Once you feel certain of your name, you must then contemplate that name for at least one year before speaking it. My name is Red Tail Hawk Soaring, and I had had red tail hawk feathers come to me through gifts and had several visions involving hawks. I felt confident that this was my true Indian name; however, I had asked to receive one more sign to be 100 percent certain.

(Note: as mentioned earlier in this chapter, hawks in Native American medicine are considered messengers of God or Great Spirit.)

The meaning of the hawk was very fitting considering the career path I was on to bring healing to the world through my gifts and talents. What wasn't clear was where I would go next, given my situation.

On this beautiful summer day, I was standing outside, leaning up against my pickup truck talking to a friend on the phone. It was a positive, upbeat conversation about overcoming obstacles and having faith and trusting in the process, knowing that we're all guided *if* we open ourselves to see the signs. Coincidentally, I was telling my friend about my explorations and visions from my attendance at the sweat lodges. I also mentioned the process I was going through to receive and validate my true Indian name. Immediately after we finished our conversation, I hung up the phone, turned around, and directly over the hillside I saw a bunch of hawks circling above! I was mesmerized as I counted ten hawks gliding together overhead—a rare sight, and not the traditional behavior of hawks. I immediately took this as a sign, and I knew it would prove important.

I enjoyed the majesty of the view for a few moments. As I internally acknowledged their presence and understood the validation they brought me regarding my Indian name, the hawks all at once broke formation, dispersed, and flew off in every direction. Wow!

Shortly following this experience, I felt as if the symbolism of the hawk was absorbing into my body, my soul. Through quiet meditation, I contemplated their messages. I could feel an indescribable power throughout my body. It was the magic of life being brought to me from the hawks and imbuing me with the power to overcome my current challenging time. I knew within my heart that I should embrace the broad vision of the hawk to see solutions for myself and my life. I am a visionary, but I had lost my way through the difficult times and was no longer seeing or thinking clearly. The hawk was teaching me that I was only as powerful as my capacity to perceive, receive, and use my abilities. I believed and knew within my heart that a tremendous opportunity was coming my way that would indeed lift me out of the rut I was stuck in. After all, there were *ten* hawks delivering the messages to me.

This was more than enough to inspire me to go forward, but I felt that there was more to it from the hawks. As I continued to sit and contemplate, I received a few more messages. The number ten, itself, was significant. It dawned on me that this was the number on the tattoo on my back. My tattoo is the Wheel of Fortune—an image from an ancient alchemical manuscript and print from 1760. This symbol is also part of the alchemical tarot deck and is, coincidently, assigned the number ten. As a chemist, the Wheel of Fortune symbol has specific meaning to me. It shows in the center, a wooden-spoked wheel with a male and a female dragon encircling the wheel, engulfing each other's tails, which symbolizes transformation. In the four corners surrounding the wheel are the four elements of the alchemical process of transmutation: earth, fire, water, and wind. The Eastern representation of this image is the yin-yang symbol, which serves as an image of contemplation and attaining a state of calm. As one begins to transform and transmute amongst the chaos of life's elements and to move to the center, one becomes grounded with oneself. It is at this point that one is able to find the center of their being and observe the rhythms of life with its ups and downs without being caught up in the whirlwind.

Most definitely I was caught up in the whirlwind of my life, which had been turned upside down. The powerful messages here were for me to return to my center and ground myself so that I may again see the direction of where these seemingly awful experiences were leading me. I accepted the realization that everything does occur for a reason and most certainly works in our favor, if only we can be patient long enough to see how.

I felt compelled to further understand the number ten—sort of a nudge from above to look up the meaning, so I did. From a numerology perspective, the number ten is associated with fate, therefore all possibilities. The number ten also returns to one (1 + 0 = 1) and represents the Universe or God, the forming of one total unit, and also a new beginning. This further cemented the message for me to find my center and reconnect with God or Great Spirit, and most importantly to know that unbounded potential was available to me.

Witnessing the beautiful pack of hawks that day and feeling the power of their message was a huge turning point during the darkest time of my life. Shortly after my experience with the hawks, I met a man that would invite me to the advisory board of a company. Through this connection and following additional signs and guidance, I've been led to form a new company that is set to revolutionize its industry. Had I not been open to the hidden power of animals, I would have never noticed the hawks circling, and I would have missed those messages in the sky.

———◆———

So you see, not only can animals send us messages and signs of confirmation, they also clearly can and will guide us through our life when we are at our lowest point. If I may be so bold, I believe the hawks saved Dr. Bill's life that summer day. The hawks needed to make an impression on Dr. Bill, and this is why they decided to appear in a pack of ten.

Next time you feel as though you've lost your hope, be open to the mystical communication shining through from animals. It just may turn your life around—literally.

The Eighth Fundamental: Choice

A key **Fundamental** to living a fulfilling life is the power of **Choice**. Choosing to embrace experiences, new perspectives, and foreign ideas impacts your ability to work through anything and shift any outcome. We all have a choice to expand our mind and believe, even when others around us don't. (While my friend and I saw a prophet in that praying mantis at the baseball game, I have no doubt other spectators saw a weird-looking bug. Oh well, their loss!)

I encourage you to choose to leverage the gifts and wisdom you can gain from your two-, four-, or eighteen-legged friends, and all those others with scales and feathers and eyes in the back of their heads. Allow their deep trust and love to speed your own healing. Just as you have a choice to remain in sadness and grief, or to embrace your loss and turn your darkness into light, you also have the choice to open your heart and mind to the mystery of the love and the language of animals.

I hope you choose to absorb their medicine whenever you need a boost. It's a choice I know you won't regret.

Tips and Considerations for Identifying Your Animal Totems

As you go about your day, appreciating the beauty of all God's creatures, great and small, consider this about the critters:

- They are indeed powerful messengers from God or Spirit.
- They're in tune with the spiritual dimensions and energies that we, as humans, don't always quite feel or understand.
- Totem animals provide guidance and wisdom, often without us even realizing.
- They are beings of unconditional love.

We have much to learn from animals. So stay open to connecting with them while they're here on earth and as they reach out and touch us from the other side. Go ahead and do some research on animal totems and see if any of them have meaning to you. And don't forget that any critter (whether a life totem or not) may pop in and out of your sight for a brief moment to deliver messages to you. They're here to help, just like your loved ones on the other side.

ᴄ 7 ᴄ

Living for Two: Who Says You're All Alone?

A h, living for two! It's been my motto ever since my sister passed when we were teens. I couldn't imagine life without her, so I decided to take her with me everywhere (and I still do)—in my heart, my soul, and my many adventures.

This chapter is about deepening your experience of life after loss and making the most of your experiences and memories. I think you'll find these stories helpful. I know I have. This first one really hit home for me.

An Angel Named Dana Reeve

Doctor Deborah Morosini of Boston, Massachusetts, is a pathologist. Her job is top-heavy in science and things that can be "proven," but she's always had strong intuitive leanings and has always prided herself on being one of those doctors with an open mind. She's been influenced, too, by the kind of fairy dust that comes out of Hollywood.

"My sister married Superman," Deborah told me. "And, nothing about their lives or deaths was ordinary." By Superman, she means Christopher Reeve. Deborah's sister Dana, an actress and singer, married the famous actor in 1992. Deborah, Dana, and their little sister, Adrienne, grew up in a tight-knit family and stayed close throughout marriages, children, careers, fame, and moving to new cities. When Christopher had the riding accident that left him paralyzed, the sisters rallied to Dana's side. When Dana and Christopher's son, Will, needed his aunties, they were there. And when Christopher died in 2004, Dana drew on the love of her sisters for support. They could always depend on each other.

What they couldn't depend on, however, was time. Dana, who had never been a smoker, learned she had stage 4 lung cancer that would eventually take her life at the age of forty-three—only four months after their mother had died of ovarian cancer and just nine months after Christopher's death.

"People feel so bad for me when they hear Dana was my sister," Deborah said. "But I tell them, 'If your sister dies, don't worry, you can definitely remain in communication. When our bond is strong with a loved one, that relationship continues. Dana sends me messages all the time. She answers every question I have, leads me to people I need to meet, and makes me laugh every day. For me, it mostly takes the form of symbols and songs, always just at the right moment in the most perfect of ways. Sometimes it almost feels like we share thoughts, although it's not as much a brain experience as more of a visceral one, manifesting through a path of incredible synchronicities.'" Dana shared a fun story about one such synchronicity:

"One day I wanted a new car that wasn't in my budget. I went to the car showroom anyway and drove off with the most unbelievable deal—where I put nothing down. As I drove off the lot, marveling at the deal and wondering if my sister had been pulling strings, a truck cut in front of me. What do you think was painted in huge letters on the back of the truck? *Dana!* That's just how it is with her. That's the norm, like having my very own Angel. It never ceases to make me laugh and cry happy tears."

I believe similar synchronicities will grace your life. Start by being open to seeing what's right in front of you.

Carry Your Love Forward

Deborah had been spellbound by Dana's crusade to educate the world about spinal cord injuries, and she wanted to do the same thing for lung cancer awareness.

"People don't know much about lung cancer," she told me. "They think you have to have been a smoker, but the reality is that 60 percent of the people diagnosed with lung cancer are nonsmokers, either having never smoked or having quit decades before. My sister never smoked. She lived a clean life. None of us had any idea that lung cancer is the leading cause of cancer death for women worldwide, killing more women each year than breast, ovarian, and cervical cancers combined. This was startling news to me. I'm a doctor. Our father is a doctor. I figured that if I was this ignorant, we had to act fast to educate the public."

To honor Dana's memory, Deborah has worked tirelessly to increase lung cancer funding. Before 2009, there was no federal money allocated for lung cancer research. In 2009, that number jumped to $20 million. In 2010, Congress appropriated $15 million more.

"Our voices are being heard," said Deborah. "When I travel the country to speak on behalf of this disease, sharing Dana's story at hospitals, with TV viewers, and for our leaders on Capitol Hill, I feel her beside me. I hear her urging me on. Her energy fuels me. Dana and Chris made a huge difference, literally changing the way the medical world both understands and treats spinal cord injuries and research. Everything from raising money for treatment to a hopeful belief in a new outcome has changed. I want to do the same thing for lung cancer. I'm a scientist, so people don't expect me to talk about my spiritual life, but there is no doubt in my mind that Dana guides every step I take to help others. There is no doubt I am furthering the work she so courageously started."

Deborah's valuable work in the world affects the lives of thousands, even millions of people—an obvious example of living for two. Her story also reveals the beautiful (though not always obvious) blessings and gifts that result from the death of a loved one. By honoring what she found so inspirational about her sister—Dana's courage to make the world a better place—Deborah keeps her sister's crusade and memory strong. Losing someone is often unbearable, but it's *always* life changing. The change can be a very positive one for you and others when you embrace the transition as Deborah has.

⸻ ◆ ⸻

Living for two is one of my favorite concepts as a way to keep our loved ones' essence alive by celebrating them. There's nothing like it for reliving cherished memories by holding onto some of the goodness of who they were. Living for two can be as simple as reading books they loved, taking a pottery class they hoped to take, or fishing on a quiet pond you once visited together.

Sometimes living for two is about bringing the *fun* back into your life. Getting you out of your comfort zone. Conquering your fears. Opening you up to things you might not otherwise try.

Skydiving for Kathy

My daredevil sister had *big* plans. She was young and wanted to do it all and see it all. Because she didn't get that chance, I've taken some wild adventures for the two of us, imagining (more like, knowing) that she's right there with me. This not only gets me up and out of the house, but it gives me courage to go for it, making these adventures all the more fulfilling.

Together, Kathy and I have ridden a hot air balloon outside of Pittsburgh; parasailed in Hilton Head, Myrtle Beach, Orlando, and Aruba; mountain climbed in Phoenix, Sedona, and Palm Springs; scuba dived in Hawaii; trekked through the Grand Canyon; sailed the open seas; ridden quads through dangerous hills; slalom water skied; snow skied down black diamonds; ridden helicopters through mountainous regions of Hawaii; and traveled through Germany, France, Italy, Mexico, the Caribbean Islands, the Bahamas, and nearly all the United States.

Kathy ached for adventure, to experience what the world had to offer. In helping to fulfill her wishes, my world expands. But the big daddy of Kathy's dreams was to go skydiving. In the hospital we made the plan to jump together if she'd lived. So, eight years after her death, it was my great pleasure to realize her dream. In a minute, we'll discuss some simple, grounded, techniques you can try in a heartbeat. But before that . . .

———◆———

It's jump time! I said, as the butterflies rippled through my stomach. I zipped up my bright orange suit, grabbed my backpack containing my chute, and hoisted myself onto the tiny propeller plane. With only enough seats for the pilot and copilot, we squeezed into the cubby hole, like sardines packed tightly inside an airtight can. My knees were practically in my mouth as I curled up in the fetal position, prepped for the long flight up.

One thousand, two thousand, three thousand, four thousand feet we climbed. I couldn't take my eyes off the altimeter attached to my suit as the engine of the plane roared like a kingdom of angry lions at the world below.

"Are you ready?" yelled the stern voice of my jumpmaster. I smiled, yelling back so he could hear me. "No turning back at this point!" I said. What I really wanted to say was, "Hell no! Take me back down, now!"

Five thousand, six thousand, seven thousand, eight thousand feet. *Oh my God, am I crazy?! Have I lost my mind?* I couldn't look out the window without getting queasy. Everything looked like it belonged to ants below. The land looked like checkerboard squares with speckles of color—a game board of life with tiny playhouses and teensy toy cars.

My mouth felt like cotton, my teeth chattered, and my body shook from anxious nerves kicking in. The two jumpmasters accompanying me in the back could only look at me and smile their devilish smiles, as if saying, "You have no idea what you're getting yourself into."

As we approached nine thousand and then ten thousand feet, Kathy was the only thing on my mind. *Oh, Kath, if only you could be here. Would you go for it, or back out?* I laughed, knowing she'd have stayed put. Living for two, my motto. And I knew she was indeed about to take the leap with me. I imagined that she'd enjoy it from the other side as much as I was.

"We're at eleven thousand feet," my jumpmaster announced. *Gulp!* The plane leveled off at speeds of about eighty to ninety miles per hour, and the pilot shut the engine down for a few brief moments as we prepared to exit. One of the jumpmasters popped up and practically threw open the door. "Whoa! That's cold!" I said. The crisp, chilled air barreled in, filling up the plane. My entire body was shivering, numb from the mixture of cold and nerves. I steadied my hands long enough to put on my goggles. So many thoughts rushed through my mind. *Will I remember everything? Will I be able to let go and actually jump? What if I get separated from my jumpmasters? What if I get separated from my jumpmasters and my chute doesn't open? Oh God and Kath, please open my chute and carry me to land!*

The two men I'd hired to flank me on either side gave me a thumbs-up and motioned for me to head to the door. "Ready?" they shouted. I smiled and nodded yes. I stood up and inched my way to the door as I watched the first jumpmaster step out onto the strut under the wing.

"Here's to you, Kath!" I said under my breath as I put one foot on the strut. I grabbed hold of the wing support bar. The first jumpmaster and I hung on in a semi-crouched position, each balancing ourselves on one foot to leave room for the second jumpmaster. The furious, hurricane-like, eighty-mile-per-hour winds whipped around us, doing their best to push me off the strut. My hands were slipping. I knew I had to make my move quickly. Panic stricken, I pushed back and forth, as instructed in class. One. Two. Three. *Jump!*

The jumpmasters leaped with me on the third push, and we began falling away from the plane. Before I knew it, I was fly-ing—arching my back, stretching my arms and legs out in an X position, my belly facing land. I couldn't have wiped the smile off my face if I'd tried.

It was amazing until the 120-mile-per-hour air blew my cheeks up like a balloon, blocking my air passage. *Oh my God, I can't breathe! Holy @#%, what do I do?* Panicked, I could feel my eyes bulge and nearly pop out of their sockets. As I stressed about how to signal hand gestures to the jumpmasters so they'd understand, I heard the still, calm voice of my beautiful sister: "Calm down. Look up toward the horizon. Close your mouth and breathe through your nose." Her voice was soft and soothing, yet firm and direct.

It worked. And the freefall took my breath away—this time in a good way. I flew like a bird. It was close to the end of a long, exhilarating day, and the horizon before me was the most beautiful orange pink, the sun about to kiss the land as it began to rest its head until tomorrow. *This is the coolest thing I've ever done or will ever do!*

At 5,500 feet, the jumpmasters motioned me. I pulled my rip cord, and my chute instantly opened and gently jerked me upright. I quickly looked up to make sure the chute opened properly, and screamed, "Woohoo!" with pure, blissful relief.

At 4,500 feet, the jumpmasters were out of sight, and I was soaring through the sky, steering my chute toward the huge orange X that stood in the empty field below. I sat back and simply took it all in. The crisp, cool breeze whistled around my body, humming a perfect, soothing song as it rocked me back and forth ever so gently through the sky. The air felt deeply fresh and rejuvenating. The scenery, an unbelievable turquoise blue sky tinged with orange and pink from the late-day sun. The emerald green treetops looked so foreign and majestic from above. The open field, a mixture of earth-tone colors weaved together perfectly, with rows and bunches of yellow and pink bushes flanking the field. The weather was a superb eighty degrees. Flawless.

I'm flying! I'm free! Free at last. Away from everyone and everything in the world! No cares or worries! No one holding me back! Hugged and nudged by the winds of Mother Nature, gliding and steering me through the open sky, I said, "This must be exactly what it's like for you, Kathy, a taste of the freedom of spirit you've experienced since leaving us."

I felt high, flying like an Angel in the heavenly sky. Every care, worry, and doubt I was carrying washed away. This bliss so silent, peaceful, and rejuvenating, was like nothing I'd ever felt before. *Oh, how I wish I could stay here forever in this moment!*

For the remainder of the trip, as I sailed back down to earth for an easy landing, back to reality, back toward the hustle and bustle of the everyday world, I vowed to carry this tremendous feeling of freedom and peace with me. And in many ways, I have. Like a trip to a foreign land that forever alters your world-view, the sense of peace and freedom I felt that day is something I draw from whenever I need it.

As you can imagine, this was the most amazing experience for me on so many levels. Certainly from the perspective that it was a great adventure that not many experience. Beyond that, it was more about connecting with my sister, feeling her near, and experiencing something I wouldn't have otherwise done had she not passed. Plain and simple, it was a pure pleasure to fly *with* Kathy!

Living for two can be done at any age or level of healing and for any reason. Although my adventures are now more in the vein of celebration, honoring your loved one can greatly help speed up your grief process and healing, or at the least make it easier to cope, as it did for Aaron.

Aaron Bakes Cookies for His Brother

Perhaps you've heard of a young boy named Aaron from Lexington Park, Maryland. Aaron now lives for two as a way to overcome his grief. He lost his twin brother, Eric, to brain cancer when the boys were only nine.

"From the womb, Aaron and Eric were inseparable," their mother, Angela, told Nate Berkus for a taping of the *Oprah* show a few years ago. "In the sonogram we saw once, they were holding hands." The boys did everything together and the loss of his brother sent Aaron into a debilitating depression in which he lost his will to live. Aaron didn't understand why this had happened, and he assumed he was doomed to the same fate.

"When do I die?" he asked his mom. "We're twins; that means I'm next."

After initial attempts with medications to ease his depression, their insightful pediatrician, Dr. Marilyn Corder, realized they weren't the answer. Instead she asked Aaron, "What do you like to do?" When he answered that he liked to cook, she said, "We're gonna cook for your brother." She gave Aaron twenty dollars and, as his first investor, asked him for a business plan. His mother said the change was immediate. "He was grinning ear to ear" on the car ride home. He made a shopping list and immediately started baking cookies in honor of Eric.

His company, Sweets by Aaron—Doughjangles, was officially started with a delivery of a tray of cookies to Dr. Corder's office, with an official list of how he'd spent her money.

Aaron and his mother bake the cookies and sell them. His big brother, Bryce, gets a stipend for helping out as well. A portion of the proceeds go to the charities that helped them when Eric was sick. His brother is never far from Aaron's thoughts as he bakes. "I think he would be proud of me," he said. "I think he'd be happy that I didn't just give up."

I spoke with Aaron's mother recently, and she's so proud of her son. So proud of the legacy he's created in the pursuit to keep his brother's memory alive. Whether he continues baking his creations for another month (he is a kid, after all) or a lifetime, he's taught the world a valuable lesson.

Who might be happy that you didn't give up? Who might love knowing that their passing opened your heart, pushed you past your fears, or enriched your life? As you know, I would prefer to bring my sister back if I could, but since I don't have that power (no one does), I had to figure out (and you do, too!) how to embrace her death and to make the most of my life . . . for me and for Kathy! She helped me figure it out. She helped me to pick up the pieces and move on, just as Eric has done for Aaron and his family. And I have no doubt your loved one will do the same for you, too.

When I'm not doing something adventurous in Kathy's memory, I'm still always open to inspiration. Sometimes I feel like eating Snyder's bar-b-q chips for no reason other than because Kathy loved them and I imagine she's having a carnal craving. I celebrate her favorite color purple by wearing it when the spirit moves me. I run through fall leaves because that's what we used to do and because I can, or I rock out to Journey because something deep inside says she'd love that right now. As I feel the music thumping through my veins, I swear I can feel her dancing behind the beats.

Sandra eats Chinese food as often as she can, because that's what her mother loved. "I feel closer to my mother in a Chinese food restaurant than just about anywhere else," she told me. "I imagine that Mom's enjoying the meal with me, which makes it fun. Who knows? Maybe she is!"

Marjory's mom loved Point Lobos on the Pacific. So when Marjory drives north from her home in Los Angeles, she takes time to stop at the state reserve on the ocean to honor her mother, who took her there as a little girl.

Jeff makes a two-hour drive at least once a month to his father's favorite spot in Maine, simply to feel closer to him and to reminisce about their time together. It's rejuvenating and healing for Jeff because this time reminds him of the life he has left to share with his own sons, to pass on the qualities that he loved so much about their grandfather.

Claire places a tape recorder by the urn of her mother's ashes and plays her mother's favorite music as she dances around her home. Claire loves music, just as her mother did. They always listened to it together as she was growing up, and Claire doesn't want to discontinue their tradition. Music helps lift Claire's mood as it whistles throughout her home, continuing to help her heal from the loss of her mom.

What adventures, or even simple activities, would you take if you knew you were protected from above? What dreams would you dare to dream? As you go through your days, think about how your life could expand if and when you let go of your fear and live for two.

Could be fun!

I can't imagine closing this chapter without including a story about a great love that stands the test of time, while also furthering worthwhile work in the world. A Rock Star/living for two example. I can think of no better role model than Coretta Scott King, the late wife of slain civil rights leader, Martin Luther King Jr.

Coretta Scott King's Dream

Martin Luther King Jr. had a dream—to see the advancement of civil rights in America and the world. He followed the teachings of Mahatma Gandhi, and his methods were always nonviolent. But that didn't stop his wife, Coretta, from worrying that her husband's enemies—which were many—wouldn't kill him.

Upon his assassination in 1968, his devoted wife made it her life's work to secure her husband's legacy and keep his dream alive. Just four days after Martin Luther King Jr.'s murder, Coretta and three of her four children returned to Memphis to lead the march her husband had organized. She took the helm of the civil rights movement when others wouldn't, and she founded the Martin Luther King Jr. Center for Nonviolent Social Change in Atlanta. Originally started in the basement of her house, the center has, according to *USA Today*, become a national shrine visited by more than 650,000 people every year.

In 2006, in an interview with NPR, Coretta said: "I understood what Martin Luther King stood for. And I felt that Martin, himself, was the noble example of what human beings could achieve. And I was hoping that we could raise up younger generations of people who would follow in Martin King Jr.'s methods—principals on non-violence and methods to bring about social change and to create the beloved community that he envisioned."

Coretta never remarried, and she died in 2006, but not before seeing her husband's birthday named a national holiday (something she pursued for over a decade), and not before becoming a tireless campaigner for world peace and being awarded the Gandhi Peace Prize by the Indian government. She was last seen in public in Atlanta at a dinner honoring her husband, and their bodies lay in rest next to each other in Atlanta, Georgia.

Just before her death, the Jewish National Fund, which plants trees in Israel, created the Coretta Scott King Forest in the Galilee region of Northern Israel. Its purpose? "Perpetuating her message of equality and peace" as well as commemorating the work of her husband.

That's some serious living-for-two action! If you're thinking that living for two has to be something so big and farfetched that you'd rather stay in the comfort of your own little life instead, I assure you the point is just to remember and honor your loved one in a way that feels comfortable to you. It isn't necessarily about saving the world, but it certainly can be. Whether big or small, this way of being lifts your spirits and makes you feel as though you can indeed save the world!

The Ninth Fundamental: Taking What Feels Right to You

In closing, allow me to point out another key **Fundamental: Taking What Feels Right to You.** I only want you to take my advice (or anyone else's, for that matter) and move forward with the things (in this chapter and this book) that feel right for you. Only you can determine, from within your heart, if my suggestions will help you heal. Only you will know if they provide you the strength you need to go where you want to go. Capturing your thoughts down in your journal, so that you can look back later to see how you worked through this difficult time, will help you know what works for you and what doesn't. In those pages you will see evidence of where you took your pain and turned it into positive energy. You will see what steps give you more juice to live out your dreams (and even, possibly, those of your loved one).

I've shared some remarkable stories with you, but I've also sprinkled a few touching, normal, everyday experiences in here to remind you that keeping your loved one's memory alive doesn't have to be a major life change. We're all spiritual beings, and connecting with Spirit should be natural. Try playing the favorite music of a loved one you miss, or making his favorite meal, or living out a dream she had that will touch people's lives. I guarantee you will also be touched and inspired by the results.

Tips and Considerations for Keeping Your Loved One's Memory Alive

I'd like to share a few techniques with you as you look to live for two (or simply keep your loved one's memory alive).

1. First, get a pen and your Angel-in-a-Pocket journal. Go to a quiet place, and give yourself some time to write down the

beautiful activities that you and your loved one used to do together. How do you feel when you think about these times? Ask yourself, would it feel good to continue doing those activities? If so, then do it. Determine **what feels right to you,** but please be sure to do only that which makes *you* happy. This in turn will bring a smile to your loved one's heart as well.

2. Next, write down what you love about the person who has passed on. Did you love her spontaneity? How he went to the movies in the middle of the day? How she picnicked in the park with her dog? Did you love how he brought flowers to your house every time he visited, just because? As you write everything you love about this person, ask yourself if you share some of these same qualities. If not, why not? Take a look within, and be more open to being carefree like your loved one, or to smile more often just because life is short.

3. As you do what you can to keep your loved one's memory alive, my guess is that your own life will also improve. Be creative with these exercises. You can think about (and write down) what your loved one dreamed about doing one day, asking yourself what you're moved to fulfill. Again, you only want to commit to that which feels right for *your* life.

4. Finally, what is it in life that you are dreaming of doing one day that somehow still hasn't happened? I think it's time for you to seriously consider your own dreams. For the sake of your loved one, and for the sake of yourself, take that leap of faith and go after that dream. Don't let fear hold you back any longer, or whatever other excuse that's had you stalled. Make a bold move! You are still here with the opportunity to do whatever you want. You *still* have the choice to live out your dreams. So go for it!

------ ◆ ◆ ------

Have fun with this! Living for two and celebrating and honoring our loved ones on the other side can be one of the most remarkable and enriching experiences of your life. I know. I live it every day.

≈ 8 ≈

Celebrating and Healing
with Your Loved One:
Rituals that Make Your
Heart Smile

You've probably noticed by now that each person has his own way of reaching out to his deceased loved one. There's no limit to the different ways in which you can find the peace, comfort, and answers you're searching for. Isn't it comforting to know that there is no right or wrong approach? By doing what feels right and following your heart and your intuition, you're sure to find your own special connection.

Whatever way you choose, let's call it a personal ritual. Your rituals can take the form of a rite of passage, a custom, a ceremony, a service, a sacrament, a repetitive behavior, or even a performance of some kind. This formal or informal act will make you feel more healed or will subsequently bring healing to a situation or another person.

If this sounds ambiguous or intimidating in any way, have no fear. You've no doubt participated in many kinds of rituals already, perhaps without even thinking about it. The only difference is that they were for the living. For instance, if you've ever attended a birthday, a shower, a baptism, a wedding, or a graduation celebration, you've participated in a ritual. Especially if you made a speech, a toast, or arrived with poems or beautifully wrapped presents for the honoree. The kind of ritual we'll be talking about in this chapter isn't much different, other than the fact that the person you're focusing on is no longer in the physical body and the gifts are more in the abstract than in the physical.

I want to get you thinking about the simple ways in which you can pay homage to the memory of your loved one, and that goes for special occasions or no occasion at all. Anything goes. This is where you get to be creative and do whatever moves you. It can be touching, soulful, sad, fun—or all of the above.

Hopefully, by the time you're done reading this chapter, you'll have a variety of ideas that inspire you to really go for it.

Anything Goes . . . Simply Follow Your Heart

Eighty-five-year-old widow Lynn drives across town to Forest Lawn Cemetery at least three times a year to pay her respects to her late husband, Robert. He's been gone now for twelve years, and she's never missed his birthday, their wedding anniversary, or the anniversary of his death—even making the trek in pouring rain, flowers in hand. When Lynn married her new husband, Andy, he went with her on occasion (before he also died)—even thanking his predecessor aloud for taking such good care of her all those years. Nowadays, when Lynn goes to Forest Lawn, she sits and talks with them both. This is Lynn's personal ritual, and it makes her feel connected.

Ellen plants a butterfly garden for her mother every spring. Her beloved mom died when she was a teenager, and her father had the vision to create a beautiful, colorful remembrance garden for his dear wife, encouraging his three daughters to pray to her amongst the flowers. Now a grown woman herself, Ellen continues the tradition—using flowers that bloom throughout the summer season and into early fall, when butterflies are most active. Each time she walks out her back door into her yard and her eyes catch sight of the luscious sunflowers, peonies, petunias, asters, nasturtiums, marigolds, and butterfly weeds and breathes in their fragrant scent, Ellen feels that much closer to the woman who gave her life. This is Ellen's personal ritual, and it makes her feel happy.

On his father's birthday every year, **Dan goes walking on the beach,** an hour's drive from his home in upstate New York. The two of them used to fish together when Dan was a boy, and being by the water allows him to feel close to his idol—who passed away while serving our country in Vietnam. Dan doesn't talk out loud much to his father during the year, but on this one occasion, he always finds it easier to open up and speak from his heart. He talks about how he's doing, what's new with the kids (his father's grandkids, whom he never met), and what he's hoping for in the coming year. Dan even asks for guidance from time to time. It doesn't matter if the weather is blustery and gray; Dan leaves feeling renewed. This is Dan's personal ritual, and it makes him feel strong and hopeful.

Visiting a cemetery, planting a garden, walking along the beach—are all simple actions, and yet extremely effective in helping these people connect and reconnect with their loved ones. It doesn't take much to keep a spirit alive or to celebrate someone's life, as these next stories reveal.

The Ritual Run Amok (aka: Letting Go)

In Alexandra's own words:
It sounds easy; like releasing your grip from holding the string of a balloon and watching it effortlessly float up into the atmosphere until it disappears into the sun. But letting go almost never happens that easily (at least not for me), even with the best of intentions.

My mother had reminded me that it was my little sister Allison's birthday. She had passed away when I was five years old, when she was only three. I remember her well, and I wanted to celebrate her short life with something beautiful and happy. I organized a colorful array of helium balloons, along with a giant multicolored butterfly balloon. Then I attached a birthday card and called my family out into the backyard to join me in sending off a little message to heaven for Allison.

My husband, Jim, questioned my choice of location, surrounded by trees, and suggested I move closer to the porch. I, in all my infinite wisdom, held steady in my decision to launch from the center of our lawn.

Up, up, up and away went the beautiful bouquet of balloons . . . until it came to rest on the top branches of our giant elm tree, where it still sits today—droopy, deflated, and stuck. The next morning I ran to the window of our loft to see if the balloons had broken free during the night. They had not. I shed a tear or two, feeling like I hadn't properly honored my little sister's memory, like I hadn't gotten it right. But as the days passed and the balloons remained, I made a conscious choice to let go of the guilt, the expectation of perfection, and remember my intention and my sense of humor.

Letting go isn't easy for me. I tend to fall in love with people, ideas, and ways of doing things, and not want to give them up. I find that the tighter I grip someone or something—it proves to be what I need to let go of the most, no matter how painful it is.

I adore Alexandra's story for a couple of reasons. First, the balloons getting "stuck" in the tree are a little like getting *connected* instead. Perhaps Alexandra's sister wanted the family to know she was there that day, and that they're forever connected.

This story is also about letting go, just as Alexandra described. Letting go seems to be one of the most difficult things for any of us to do. But God knows best. As we loosen our grip, and the expectations we have for how something should or shouldn't be, we let Him do His job for us.

The Garden Goodbye

Back in Chapter 1, my friend the artist Elizabeth Murray shared the way in which she uses the practice of automatic dialoguing to communicate with her dead husband, Gerald.

Elizabeth is a medicine woman, a modern-day priestess. People come from all over the world to work with her, flying into picturesque Carmel-by-the-Sea, California, for healing ritual workshops and intensive weekends or weekdays spent by the sea. As the author of *Cultivating Sacred Space: Gardening for the Soul*, Elizabeth not only knows a thing or two about the healing power of herbs, plants, and flowers, but she takes people on one heck of a nature walk. Clients fly into Monterey airport feeling stuck and scared, and they leave feeling rejuvenated and freed. This is Elizabeth's passion.

It is fitting, then, that Elizabeth performed a garden ritual wake when Gerald died. As she told me, and so beautifully detailed in her book, *Cultivating Sacred Space*, Elizabeth performed, without realizing it, a time-honored ritual from Mexico. There, when someone you love dies, you make a fire and sit with the fire all night, feeding it and gathering around the flames as you talk about the person who died. It's thought of as a way to comfort one another as you light a path for the soul who has been called away.

"We gathered baskets and filled them with offerings," she told me, "using rosemary (which is about remembrance), bamboo (seen as a connection of heaven and earth), sage (for purification), and pieces of cedar (for clarity)." Friends were invited to place these sacred offerings into the fire. People sang songs and told stories about Gerald, followed by a feast of his favorite foods. Since Gerald had loved making his own fireworks, his friends did the same and set them off at dusk. "We sent his spirit soaring into the starlit heavens that night," she said. "With the music and the love and the food and the joy, it truly was a celebration of his life."

Because Elizabeth is so tapped in to the practice of ritual, I asked her if she'd ever experienced a Rock Star ritual. Of course, she had. It's our hope that this true tale gets you excited about the unlimited possibilities awaiting you when dealing with the Divine!

Honoring Saint Therese Leads to a Miracle

Elizabeth lives in a historic home in one of the original structures that launched the Carmel/Monterey Peninsula as a famous artist community (the home Gerald told her he loved in the automatic dialoguing letter from Chapter 1). Jack London used to read his manuscripts out loud in this house!

But by the time Elizabeth found the rambling structure and its overgrown garden, it was in disrepair. Structural engineers had declared it dangerous—worse, even—impossible to repair. "When a cat walked upstairs, the whole house shook," Elizabeth said. But she was determined to buy the home and return it to its former glory as a sanctuary for artists in this era. Once Elizabeth saw the place, she couldn't release her vision. She'd actually been searching with three realtors for over four years for a home like this—something large enough to teach in, show her art in, and create her art in, with a large garden and a few shacks on the property she could renovate into rentals to help fund her creative pursuits. She'd searched and searched, and prayed to God and Gerald often about how to find such place, envisioning that it would be an old artist's home.

"Two of the realtors dropped me," she explained, "saying, 'This is ridiculous. You will never find this house.'" But a psychic told her she would indeed find the house and that it would be on a street with some kind of a saint name.

Elizabeth found this home—on Ave Maria Drive. The trouble was, she didn't have the money to save the house. It was twice her budget. The garden, however, called to her (just as Monet's garden in France, from Chapter 1, had decades earlier). It desperately needed restoring, and she felt compelled by a deep longing to be the one to take that on. Elizabeth had been waiting four years already for money to come out of probate from Gerald's estate, and it hadn't yet closed. And, she hadn't yet sold her own house in order to come up with the down payment. She was running out of time, as other buyers were vying for the property and would soon tear the house down.

"I used to have conversations in my mind with the dead artists who had previously enjoyed the home," she told me. "I gave them a job—asking that they literally hold the ceiling up until we could get the money to buy the place, not to mention the steel support beams in place to save the structure. Since the whole thing was sinking by seven inches or more, this was no small request. They had their work cut out for them." What a way to ask for help! I believe those on the other side love being summoned for jobs like this.

One evening Elizabeth and a friend drove to the Monastery of Saint Therese in the Carmel Highlands—a silent monastery where the nuns don't speak. Therese had died at the age of twenty-four in 1897, with a great desire to travel, so for whatever reason, her relics were touring the world and made a visit to the place named as her first monastery.

Elizabeth is not Catholic, but she is deeply spiritual and thought it would be a powerful ritual to visit the monastery because Saint Therese's relics (bones) were coming that night. They traveled around the world in a beautiful box tomb—the most exquisite type of Victorian doll house–looking structure you've ever seen "times a million," she said, "with a glass top." It weighed around 350 pounds.

It was pouring wildly that night. "A crazy, stormy night," Elizabeth said. "No one usually goes to this monastery, but earlier there had been thousands of people parking and walking up the long, long driveway to the monastery. By the time we got there, just minutes before they were closing, nearly everyone had gone home because of the voracity of the storm."

The nuns were at the altar singing when Elizabeth and her friend sat down. The relics were on the altar. While kneeling and praying, Elizabeth's friend elbowed her and whispered: "Go show her pictures of the house. Ask her to help you."

"I can't do that," answered Elizabeth. "She's busy; she helps sick people. I can't do that."

"No, she's really powerful," said her friend. "That's nothing for her. Go ask her." Elizabeth had left the photos at her own home, on an altar with a lit candle and written prayers to "both sides of the realm" to help her secure the house.

They walked up to the altar and envisioned the house while Elizabeth prayed: "I don't want to disturb you, Saint Therese. But if this isn't too much, and if you think I should, and if it's okay, it would be so lovely if you could help me with this. Please don't even help me if I won't be able to keep the house up. And, please give me advice." Elizabeth needed guidance because the next day was the deadline to tell her one remaining realtor if she was going to be able to get the money for the down payment.

By the time they left the church, the enormous storm had completely lifted, revealing a sky full of stars.

"I heard this voice," Elizabeth told me. "The voice said, 'Keep it simple, tell the truth, and ask for help.' So, I hatched a plan. I would tell the truth and keep it simple by telling the owners that I didn't have enough money, that I couldn't get a bridge loan, and that I needed their help. If they would let me borrow $250,000 in order to give it back to them for the down payment, I could buy myself both time to get the money, and the house. I told my realtor about my plan and she said I'd be 'blowing my chance' for sure. 'You'll lose the house.'

"'Then so be it,' I said. "Around that time a friend called me with a gift. She had loads of historic roses she wanted to give me for my new house. Catholic lore says that when Saint Therese answers your prayers, you will get unexpected roses."

As the Divine would have it and as you might guess, the owners loved Elizabeth's plans to restore the house to its original state, and they decided to take a gamble on her. Their faith was rewarded. Soon after they loaned her the money, her own house sold *and* she got her inheritance from Gerald's estate. The house was hers, her debt to the owners was repaid, and the renovations went beautifully.

Elizabeth's home and garden, complete with many roses, is a sanctuary for artists throughout her grateful community.

So you see, rituals take the form of celebration, asking for help (thus opening the lines of communication between worlds), or the more everyday, common ritual of simply reminiscing. Whatever it may be, your ritual is yours; it's special, and it leaves a lasting impression. Some of my favorites entail those that help heal your heart and clear the way for easier two-way communication. Like these that bring forgiveness.

Forgiveness Healing Ritual

My friend Ana Holub is a world-class forgiveness expert and author who lives and works out of Mount Shasta, California.

Her work takes her many places, even to San Quentin State Prison, where she works with male prisoners to find forgiveness in the worst of circumstances. Needless to say, Ana's work is deeply healing.

Ana and I were talking about this chapter, and I asked her to share some of her enormous wisdom with you—and to write it up in such a way that you could feel that you were together, performing a forgiveness ritual for your loved ones. I hope you can take in the spirit of love in her words, and maybe even imagine that you're doing this exercise in a meadow on the majestic Mount Shasta—all that much closer to God and the Angels themselves.

Ao you'll witness, Ana's insight is perfect for the closing chapter of this book because not only will you walk away with key considerations for healing and forgiving yourself and others, her approach also pulls together much of what we've been speaking about throughout the book—the fundamentals to living the most spiritually fulfilled life possible.

In Ana's own words:

Joan is my favorite other-side friend. She was a dancer, performer, choreographer, and my mother-in-law (and still-loving, ex-mother-in-law) before she passed away in 2009, with friends and family by her side.

Joan showed me what a good death looks and feels like, and to me, it was miraculous. After experiencing plenty of grief and loss after the deaths of both my parents, Joan's transition healed something deep within me. Even during her last days, she was fearless, gentle, loving, and receiving of love. After she died, I had the honor of washing her body, anointing it with holy oils, dressing her in bright purple and teal, and praying for her with five other women. Her memorial was packed with friends who laughed, cried, sang, and danced in her honor.

Since that time, Joan visits me often, sometimes bearing gifts. The last time was around Christmas, when she led me to a gorgeous cashmere sweater in deep blue, in a recycle shop for ten dollars. Thanks, Joan!

I asked Joan to help me write up this piece on rituals for Deborah and her readers—you. Actually, it's sort of ironic, since Joan didn't cotton to long-winded ceremonies with lots of airy-fairy stuff. So, we'll make it short, simple, and to the point. Very healing, nonetheless.

Use this ritual for healing relationships with loved ones **where there's still some unfinished pain or sadness for you.** The key point to remember is that you're going to keep the love, and let go of the rest.

Moving Beyond the Pain of the Past

1. **Take Stock.** Give yourself time to reflect and write in your Angel Journal. Acknowledge all aspects of your relationship—the good, the bad, the sublime, and the horribly ugly. Learn from all of it. Look deeply, and ask, *What did I learn from both the difficulties and the joys I experienced with my loved one?* Write down the lessons you gained, leaving nothing out. Remember that every aspect has its perfect message for you about life and love. Seen in this context, even what seems like heartbreak has its treasures. Find them.

2. **Release Regrets and Sorrows.** Go to a healing place, by yourself or with a trusted friend or counselor. If possible, go to a private place you feel connected to in nature. If you stay inside, make an altar or sacred space in your home for this work. If you like, you can make a fire and burn your writings. Or you may prefer to keep them as part of your life history.

    The main thing is to release any regret, fear, sadness, anger, disillusionment, and confusion about your relationship with your loved one. You can do this by being very, very honest with what you're feeling, including allowing tears or rage to surface. Make some noise if you need to and let yourself express. (Sound familiar? We spoke of this in Chapter 2.) Say anything, out loud, especially things you never had the guts to say to your loved one before. As waves of emotion come up and out of you, offer them to the Great Spirit, God, Goddess, or whatever you choose to name the Divine. Call upon Angels, masters, saints, or ancestors if it feels right. They're happy to help as soon as you ask!

Release all suffering from your body, emotions, memories, and mind *so that you can be free*. Breathe it out with each exhale, long and slow. It's time to forgive by unwinding your pain and letting it go. Give it as a gift to God with humbleness and simplicity. Any heartbreak can be over as soon as you lay down your burdens and breathe them out of your body. This takes Trust, Honesty, Openness, and Willingness. Trust that Spirit can carry the pain away, just as your loved one was carried by the Mystery to another dimension. This release is essential for you. It's a gift you give yourself so you can heal and recover the love you both share.

3. **Keep the Love.** Now that you've reviewed, unwound, and let go of your knots of pain, all that's left is a pure soul connection with your loved one. Take some time to breathe it in, using your inhale to wash love and light throughout your body and mind. When you're ready, reach to your loved one with gratitude, acknowledging your eternal bond. Tell the person how you feel, out loud, because his spirit is present with *you now*.

Get used to being completely seen and deeply loved by your soul friend as you rest together in Spirit. Now that you've got a confidant on the other side, welcome her as an ally whose unique access to cosmic synchronicity will lighten you up and bring you joy.

4. **Stay Open to the Future.** From now on, you'll be receiving messages of support from your soul buddy. Just as I receive from Joan, and Deborah receives from Kathy, cool little gifts will come your way. Perhaps they'll come in the form of jokes, inner winks, intuitive conversations, or sweaters. Maybe they'll be life-changing miracles and exciting new opportunities—who knows?

Relax and enjoy your eternal connection. You've made room for wonder, mystery, and everlasting, healing love. Life is on your side—on both sides of the veil—and now you'll be awake and eager to receive it.

And, as Deborah has told you so beautifully before, be sure to send gratitude and blessings to your loved one. Relationships are a two-way street!

————◦◆◦————

I love that Ana took the time to bring a piece of her God-given work to share here, as we discuss the crucial process of grieving and healing. I couldn't have said it better. I will add that as you follow the advice throughout all the chapters of this book, I know you'll work through your grief and find the love, joy, and happiness awaiting you in your life.

Ana's insight is a true gift, as is this next offering—a poem she wrote for Joan. Perhaps it will inspire you to write your own poetry, even if you've never tried that before. Writing poetry or letters to a loved one, or about a loved one, is yet another powerful ritual that can provide enormous healing—for the author and reader alike.

For Joan
My heart is so still,
so empty.

You showed me that
today can be a
good day to die.

Showed me the passing
that is gentle and whole.
You came to flight softly,
with honor.

Inside your last breath
you swallowed the mountain
your open eyes gazed
into open sky.

Once again, you show me
time is nothing.

You choreographed a flawless dance
moving, flowing
with friends and family
spikenard from Jerusalem
lavender from the front yard
prayers in gold,
purple, and teal.

With your beauty, I heal
a thousand ugly deaths.

Once again, you are the elder
tap dancing your way
to freedom,
for after all, as you know,
the show must go on.

—Ana Holub, September 2, 2009

The Memorial Prayer

When my coauthor Linda Sivertsen learned the heartbreaking news that her mother, Joanne Tisch, had terminal cancer, she raced to write her a letter for Mother's Day to let her know what a wonderful mother she was and would always be. Linda gave it to her mom before she died and then read it aloud at her mother's memorial.

The following is an excerpt of that letter:

Dearest Mom,
I thought you might want to know a few of the reasons I love you—past and present.
I love hearing your voice (nobody has it but you).
I love the way you always answered all of my questions as a kid.

And the way you cooked for us, always yummy, and had breakfast and lunch ready before we went to school.
And the way you drove me everywhere.
And read to me.
And waited for me to come home from school, and listened to my day with interest.
And told Dad not to make me clean my room.
I love how you took me to the park.
And comforted me when it rained and we couldn't go.
I love how you tucked me in at night, every night.
And how you would come home late sometimes, and hug me with your fake fur, so soft.
I love the way you ask for guidance, and admit you're not perfect.
And the way you are eating healthy foodstuffs and doing your affirmations.
I love the way you send my son little notes and packs of gum.
And, football- and basketball-shaped Easter chocolates.
And how you write us letters beginning with "Dear Dolls."
And how you type labels on the tapes you send us.
I love how you save (and recycle) water and foil and plastic bags and paper towels.
And how you always have fresh flowers in the house, and roses in the garden.
And how you taught me to love planting things.
And, cooking and cleaning and mothering.
I love how you are such a good host at dinner parties.
And how you laugh at Dad's jokes, time and time again.
I love how you would wave at me from the front porch, or from the road, depending on how long I'd be gone.
And how you'd make me salad for breakfast.
And showed me how to get up each morning with a smile.
And how to pray at night before bed.
And how to appreciate the rain with all my heart, putting all the indoor plants outside to have a drink.
I love how you'd shop at the funky health food stores (that are now all the rage).

*And make lumpy carob-chip, oatmeal cookies that tasted
better than the smooth kind.
I love how your little nose gets tan in the sun.
And how you called me "Freckle Nose."
And how you helped me to love myself, knowing that what-
ever I did, my mom loved me.
Cause that's what you do best . . . love.
I hope you can love yourself as much as others love you.
Because the world is a much better place with you in it!
Those are a few of the things I love about you, but not all.
Words are never enough, ever.*

*Forever,
Linda*

Although Linda didn't have much more time to be with her mother, this letter helped her tell her mother what she wanted her and needed her to know, and it kept her memories for safekeeping—like a written time capsule. It's been many years since her mother's death, and Linda's convinced she would have forgotten some of these sacred details by now. You, too, can make a list of the things you love about anyone, alive or on the other side, to keep forever.

------◆------

I'd like to leave you with one final ritual to use as you work through your grief or through any challenging situation in your life. You'll feel the power of this the very first time you try it.

The Flyaway Ritual

It's easy to get so caught up in our worries, fears, doubts, sadness, guilt, shame, and anger that we no longer see or think clearly. You may even find yourself questioning your loved one's death; consumed by what it must have been like for him or what you could have or should have done differently to keep it from happening. I call this the fog. When it descends, you lose sight of the blessings all around you. If you find yourself stuck in a grieving rut or worried to the point of distraction, know that you're only hurting yourself and holding yourself back. It doesn't take long to recognize that being in this energy doesn't feel good. Make a choice to move away from this negative space. Shift the vibe. Release that which no longer serves you (believe it or not, feeling guilty doesn't serve your highest purpose).

Get yourself to a place of love, joy, and compassion for yourself, your loved ones on the other side, and those still here with you on earth. Make a conscious effort—you owe it to yourself! Because much of what you feel when you walk through life with a heavy heart is not true or real. Those feelings are coming from a place of fear, guilt, or sadness. When you're ready to accept the situation and let it go for good, try this Flyaway method. My clients have had great success with it. Maybe you will, too!

1. Imagine holding a big, purple helium balloon by a string.
2. Place your worry, doubt, fear, or guilt (the entire situation) inside of your balloon.
3. Now envision seeing the situation inside the balloon as you continue holding the string.
4. Envision walking outside and letting go of the string.
5. Watch as the balloon flies up into the sky, farther and farther away, until you can no longer see even a speck in the sky.
6. Say a prayer or set an intention that this situation is now resolved, complete, or dissolved.
7. Take a few big, deep breaths and feel the joy in your body now that this issue is done. Have faith and believe with all your heart that all is resolved. Never question. Never waiver. Believe and have faith!
8. Finally, do your best to leave it alone forever, keeping the following in mind if those worrisome, fearful thoughts creep back into your head:
   a. Make a conscious effort to let those thoughts go when they surface or pop into your mind. Living a life *free of* ego-based emotions (i.e., worry, guilt, etc.) is only one thought away. Truly. It's a choice. The choice is yours.

b. Turn the mind chatter off when it dumps these heavy feelings atop your shoulders. Because fear feels cruddy, commit to shift your focus to a place of love by reconnecting with Spirit or your loved ones through meditative practices. Meditation is one way to reconnect with God and to tune in to your heart and soul.

This ritual is a powerful expression to your psyche and the Divine that you are ready to be free and happy from this point on.

Remember, being honest with yourself, feeling your emotions, and processing them will better allow you to let them go. Reconnecting with Spirit and your loved ones on the other side will fill your heart with love, lifting you up energetically and providing you the faith, courage, and strength to conquer your grief and challenges once and for all.

The Tenth Fundamental: Love

The last **Fundamental** that I will cover is **Love.** My favorite.

In my humble opinion, love is indeed the most important fundamental. And I'm not talking about being in love with someone else; I'm talking about the love you have for yourself. Love starts at home—from within you. One of the key steps to standing strong, no matter what life brings, is the love you have for yourself. Loving you for you. Accepting yourself for who you are, what you do, what you have (or don't), and loving yourself regardless. When you truly and fully love yourself, you're building your life on the strongest foundation there is.

Love is everything, and love does conquer all. Love brings with it happiness, inspiration, strength, confidence, courage, faith, and so many more positive energies that are needed to work through any loss or difficult situation.

My recommendation to you is to do the best you can to find the love for yourself within your heart. When you do this, everything else miraculously falls into place.

You may wonder how to begin loving yourself. First, start by writing down what you like about yourself. Then when you are ready, work your way to the list of what you *love* about yourself.

This can be a difficult task, so if you need help getting started, ask someone close to you to describe you and your finest qualities. Carry your list with you to remind yourself of your greatest talents and characteristics. Put them in your wallet, where you see them every time you spend money. Loving yourself is a process and requires effort to embrace the unconditional love you already have inside. It's innate within each of us; we simply need to stoke the fire.

Tips and Considerations as You Go on Your Way

Finally, I'd like to take one last moment to reiterate some of the important tips and considerations for connecting to loved ones on the other side and living a more spiritually fulfilled life.

- Have faith that every experience in your life is a necessary stepping-stone for all the good that's ahead of you now. Be open to recognizing the blessings in *every* experience. In time you will ultimately see these gifts, even from awful situations.

- Remember that you cannot heal until you feel! Process your emotions and find an outlet for each one. Only then can you begin to heal.

- There's no right or wrong way in which to grieve; nor is there a specific timeframe to complete the bereavement process. Work through it in a way that feels natural to you.

- Always do the best you can to accept yourself, your life, your experiences, your challenges, your emotions, and that your loved one is no longer here in the physical sense. Know and believe in your heart that your loved one is *closer than you think*, spiritually.

- Have faith, and relax your mind and body in order to be open to and aware of any divine messages coming your way. Be open to receiving theses signs in any manner they are delivered. Whether they are through Rock Star moments or Subtle Signs, both are powerful, life changing, and healing.

- Don't forget to ask for help from your loved ones above. Asking for help is a sign of strength. The best part is they love lending us a hand when it doesn't interfere with a life lesson we must learn on our own.
- When you're having a down day or a difficult time moving beyond your grieving, stop and ask yourself the following questions (sometimes it's questions like these that help us snap out of it):
  - What would my loved one want me to do?
  - Does he want me to be sad?
  - Does she want to see me giving up and not living my life?
  - Wouldn't it make him happy to see me smile again?

  Your loved ones do not want to see you suffer. And, more importantly, being happy and living your life to the fullest doesn't mean you don't love and miss your loved one terribly. It's actually the reverse. It shows your loved one just how much you love them, love yourself, and love life. So live on!
- Remember to open your heart to the beauty of God's critters and the powerful ways in which animals touch your heart or deliver messages to you.
- Don't forget the use of your Angel Journal to:
  - Capture those moments when your loved one may be reaching out to you.
  - Write letters or poems to your loved one letting him know how you feel—no matter what those emotions may be (sadness, anger, guilt, happiness, loneliness, and so on).
  - Jot down the qualities of your loved one that inspire you to be a better person.
  - Use your journal in any manner that helps you work through the grieving process and build the beautiful spiritual connection with your loved one that I believe we're all meant to have.

- Celebrate and honor your loved one through your own personal ritual. This is a special activity just for you and your loved one. It can be anything—visiting his favorite place, making her the yummy apple pie that she loved baking, planting a garden in his honor, or simply taking a moment each night to look up to the sky and blow her a kiss. Do whatever feels right to you and makes your heart smile or sing. It will certainly bring a smile to your loved one's heart as well.
- During all of this process, always remember to take care of yourself—it's what your loved one would want you to do. Write a list of your favorite things to do or the hobbies that drive your passion. Do something for yourself every day; even if only for a brief moment. And work toward your dreams; your loved one will be cheering you on from above.

———⋅◆⋅———

As this book—my love letter to my sister and all of our loved ones on the other side—comes to a close, I want to thank you for joining me on this journey. I am humbled and honored that you have spent your valuable time with me. Always trust that your loved ones really are *closer than you think.*

Please know that I cherish hearing from you and learning of your stories. I would love to include details of your magical communications in future books and projects—to inspire others with how you've turned your pain into peace.

I wish you all the joy, light, and laughter in the world. I thank you for making my journey with Kathy one of the most rewarding experiences any girl could be fortunate enough to have.

Blessings to you and yours,

Deborah
deb@painintopeace.com

Acknowledgments

Deborah's Acknowledgments

I am forever grateful for the number of family members and friends who have supported me along my journey of writing this book. I've gained many new friends while being divinely guided to share a part of me and my life as it exists ever since my sister's transition in 1987. I'm very thankful to everyone who so openly shared their stories with me and allowed me to share them with you. This book would not be what it is without all of you.

I'd like to acknowledge and send a special thank-you to several very special people in my life. My wonderful, handsome, precious boys, Evan and Aaden. Every day you touch my heart in a way that words can't describe. I'm eternally grateful for the blessing of you both. I pray you will always know, feel, and see how beautiful life is and how precious you are to me and to this world. Most of all, I give you my love and support forever. Thank you for reminding me of the purity and unconditional love we are all made of. You both are an inspiration to me, and I'm honored to be your mom. I know you'll always bring greatness to this world.

To Jim Heneghan, a wonderful man and father to Evan and Aaden. I could not have done this without your unconditional support since I started this journey. You believed in me from day one, and I can't thank you enough. I will never forget the sacrifices made and the support during the many long evenings and nights working to meet deadlines. Your input and guidance has been invaluable. You've helped me to see beyond my own little world. I'm forever grateful to you.

To my fabulous, awesome parents, Ed and Pat. Thank you for always believing in me and supporting me for *all* decisions I've made in my life, even those you didn't necessarily agree with. Your love and support means the world to me. Your strength and courage to handle life's experiences is a true inspiration. You both are amazing, and I'm honored to be your daughter.

To my beautiful, loving, big sister, Cindy, who is very special to me in so many ways. We've been through a lot in our lives, but never once did we leave each other's side. You're amazing! Thank you for *you* and for *everything* you do for me in every area of my life. I will always be grateful for your help, support, guidance, and love. I wouldn't be who I am today if you weren't in my life. Love you tons and tons!

To my very best friend and soul sister, Jules, who entered my life over ten years ago. You've taught me more than I can ever thank you for. You are a true Angel here on earth, and I will always be grateful for our talks, our secrets, and those emotional roller-coaster rides, but most of all for our acceptance of each other for who we are. Thank you for being my inspiration and cheering section along the path to write this book, but also along my spiritual journey. You're the best!

To the rest of my beautiful family and friends—you are all are very special to my heart. I wouldn't be who I am without the love and support you've shown me throughout my life. I'll always cherish the closeness we have. *We are family!*

Linda Sivertsen, my coauthor and forever friend. This book would not be what it is today if it wasn't for you, your creativity, and your tremendous talent. You and your beautiful, gifted writing assistant, Natalie Kottke, helped me put together the winning book proposal that landed me the deal with Hampton Roads and Red Wheel/Weiser. You helped bring life to this book. You are a true Angel brought to me from above. Thank you so much for those long days, evenings, and nights. Most of all, thanks for you. You rock, sista!

My heartfelt thanks goes out to those of you who shared your powerful, beautiful stories with me and with the readers of this book. I'm eternally grateful to you for sharing a part of your lives with us. You've touched my heart so deeply with your stories, and I know you'll do the same for everyone else. *Thank you* from my entire heart and soul for your caring heart. I'm very blessed to know each of you.

To all of the Breckinridge babes, beauties and my forever soul sisters: Linda, Natalie, Dana, Elaine, Lynda, and Teresa. I'll never forget our week together in Colorado. You are all an inspiration to me. Thank you for your encouragement, ideas, support, guidance, and love for my writing project, which you now hold in your hands.

Caroline, Ali, Bonni, Susie, and everyone at Red Wheel/ Weiser, thank you so much for seeing the gifts and blessings in this book and placing your confidence in me. Thank you for your continued guidance and input throughout the process of writing, editing, and finalizing the book. It is a true pleasure to work with each of you!

To my cohost and friend, Dr. Bill Clark, you've been a tremendous inspiration to me as I journey down my own spiritual path. You've taught me so much each week on our radio show, and you've helped me to understand more about the true me. I'll never forget the support you've shown me. You are a true Angel on this earth, and I'm blessed to know you.

Most of all, thank you, Kathy, my beautiful sister, my Angel friend, and my inspiration for all that I do and for all that I am. This book is here because of *you*. You're amazing! Thank you, God and all of our loved ones who have transitioned, and all heavenly guides and Angels who have continuously guided me and led me down my own spiritual path. I appreciate life so much more because you've sprinkled a bit of heaven upon me. I'm blessed to be able to share this stardust with everyone who reads this book!

Hugs and blessings to all!

Linda's Acknowledgments

It's been my honor to work with Deborah on this blessing of a book. I'll never forget our first meeting, in the mountains of Breckenridge, Colorado, with our writing retreat group. Thanks to Elaine, Teresa, Dana, Lynda, and Natalie for supporting Deb in her embrace of this sacred topic. Her heartfelt desire to share Kathy and their continuing relationship with others touched us all. Big love to everyone in this book who shared their stories, and to those who make every day a blessing for me—my best friend Diane Chandler; my sister and her husband, Carol and Bill Allen; our angels Dorothy Allen, and Al and Joanne Tisch; my son, Tosh Sivertsen (and his beautiful "sis" Hayli Metter), and the love of my life, Larry Metter. Here's to our journey together—whether here or "there," may our bonds be eternal.

Resources

For more information about **Deborah Heneghan** and her company, Closer Than You Think, LLC, please visit *www.closer thanyouthinkthebook.com* and *www.journeytospiritual truth.com*. You can also submit your own story for consideration for future books.

Dr. Bill Clark, PhD, author, inspirational spiritual teacher, and cohost with Deborah Heneghan on their radio show, *Journey to Spiritual Truth—Finding Joy and Love Through Life's Experiences* (*www.journeytospiritualtruth.com/radio.html*). For more information on retreats, workshops, speaking engagements, and finding your way through your journey to spiritual truth, visit *www.journeytospiritualtruth.com*.

Zen DeBrucke, author, inspirational leader, cofounder of Smart Soul Academy, author of *The Smart Soul: Discovering Your Internal Guidance System, Transform Anxiety into Fulfillment and Success*, which provides the practices to understand your own internal guidance system. For more information, visit *www. zendebrucke.com*.

Guy Dusseault, author of *Signs from Our Loved Ones: Our Son Billy*. Visit *www.oursonbilly.com* to read about the inspiration, peace, and comfort Guy and his family receive from their loved one on the other side. Visit Guy's blog at *www.signsfromourlovedones.wordpress.com*.

Alexandra Hill, fashion-journalist-turned-blogger. Alexandra uses her experiences as an editor, wife, mother, and occasional tennis player to describe her everyday life with her newly discovered spirituality (including Guides and Angels) with self-deprecating humor and an occasional hanky. Her blog can be found at *www.stumblingintospirituality.blogspot.com*.

Ana Holub, Clear Path to Peace. Ana offers spiritual counseling, forgiveness counseling, emotional healing, anger management, and reconciliation to strengthen and enliven your experience of inner peace and balance in the world. For more information about Ana and her services visit *www.anaholub.com*.

Susan Kimutis, author of *Receiving Birth*, a book about her experiences with the process of adoption. Susan is also the author of an amazing, inspirational blog which touches the hearts of so many who have lost loved ones, particularly children. For more information and to read her blog, visit *www.susankimutis.com*.

Deborah Morosini, MD, lifelong intuitive, sister of the late Dana Reeve. Deborah is an inspirational speaker, lung cancer activist, and molecular pathologist working in oncology. She began HeartStorm coaching in 2011 to explore and share her intuitive process with others who are seeking to engage synchronicity for healing and guidance. Visit *www.deborahmorosini.com*.

Elizabeth Murray, author, photographer, and keynote speaker best known for helping restore Monet's gardens and photographing them in Giverny, France annually for over twenty-five years. Murray is a bestselling author of books including: *Monet's Passion* and *Cultivating Sacred Space*. She is a recognized expert on creativity, spirituality, gardens, ritual, beauty, and life mapping. For more information on personal retreats, workshops, keynote talks, or art, visit: *www.elizabethmurray.com* or email emurray@elizabethmurray.com.

Angie Pechak Printup, author of *He Blew Her a Kiss: Inspirational Stories of Communication from Loved Ones Who Have Passed*. Visit *www.heblewherakiss.com* to read stories from others who have had after-death-communication experiences. You can share your story there as well.

Rev. Marjorie Augustine Rivera, internationally known and respected psychic medium. If you are unsure that the messages and signs you are receiving are indeed from your loved ones on the other side, or if you want validation of these signs, Rev. Marjorie is a very gifted, wonderful psychic medium who can connect to your loved ones and help you connect directly. Visit her website at *www.moonstonemediums.com*.

Linda Sivertsen, coauthor with Deborah Heneghan, book proposal doctor, author whisperer, agent connector, idea fairy, and cheerleader of creativity for writers of all genres—and every gold-plated publishing dream. In addition to authoring and coauthoring eight books—including *Generation Green: The Ultimate Teen Guide to Living an Eco-Friendly Life*, *Lives Charmed: Intimate Conversations with Extraordinary People*, and the *New York Times* bestseller *Harmonic Wealth: The Secret of Attracting the Life You Want*—Linda's ghostwriting, coaching, and curatorial talents are sought after by Emmy and Oscar Award winners, business leaders, celebrities, and new writers around the world. Find her and her Carmel Writing Retreats at *www.bookmama.com*.

Bobby E. Smith, PhD, author of *The Will to Survive: A Mental and Emotional Guide for Law Enforcement Professionals and the People Who Love Them* with coauthor Linda Sivertsen, and author of *Visions of Courage: The Bobby Smith Story*. Bobby is the director of Louisiana State Police Trooper Assistance Program and the president of Visions of Courage, Inc. Visit his website at *www.visionsofcourage.com*.

Angela Brown Ware, author of *One Day We'll Dance Again*, and owner of Sweets by Aaron—Doughjangles, a company started with her son Aaron in honor and memory of Aaron's twin, Eric, who passed away from brain cancer. Please visit *www.doughjangles.com*.

About the Author

JANE ENGS PHOTOGRAPHY

Deborah Heneghan is an inspirational spiritual teacher, author, intuitive, Reiki certified healer, and Angel worker and has been on her spiritual path for many years. She is also a professional businesswoman and has worked as a software architect for over nineteen years.

Deborah has helped thousands of people work through the grieving process from the loss of a loved one, through her teleseminars, personal coaching, spiritual workshops and retreats, and radio show.

Deborah has also been a guest on many radio and TV shows including: *The Balancing Act*, which airs on Lifetime Television; *Meet the Experts with Arielle Ford*, which has aired on CBS, NBC, ABC, and FOX; Dr. Carole Lieberman's radio show *Dr. Carole's Couch*; and *News for the Soul* radio; among others.

You can visit with Deborah at *www.closerthanyouthinkthebook .com*.

About the Coauthor

Writing coach and award-winning, *New York Times* best-selling coauthor Linda Sivertsen has been midwifing stories since 1998. Writers, like Deborah, who come to her transformational writing retreats in Carmel-by-the-Sea often have no idea what to write about but leave with ideas that become book deals—like this one. Through Linda's experiences of caring for her parents when they were dying of cancer, she has developed a profound understanding of the process of grieving while staying open to inspiration and guidance.

Linda lives just north of Los Angeles with her dreamy man and their two precious pups. She can be reached at *www.bookmama.com*.